SOMALIA

SOMALIA

TITLES IN THE MODERN NATIONS OF THE WORLD SERIES INCLUDE:

Brazil
Canada
China
Cuba
Egypt
England
Germany
Greece
India
Ireland
Italy
Japan
Kenya
Mexico
Russia
Somalia
South Africa
South Korea
Spain
Sweden
The United States

SOMALIA

BY SALOME C. NNOROMELE

LUCENT BOOKS
P.O. BOX 289011
SAN DIEGO, CA 92198-9011

For Patrick, Nmeli, Christa, and Hannah

Library of Congress Cataloging-in-Publication Data

Nnoromele, Salome, 1967–
    Somalia / by Salome Nnoromele.
        p.   cm. — (Modern nations of the world)
    Includes bibliographical references and index.
    Summary: Examines the land, people, and history of Somalia and
discusses its state of affairs and place in the world today.
    ISBN 1-56006-396-3 (lib. : alk. paper)
    1. Somalia—Juvenile literature. [1. Somalia.] I. Title.
II. Series.
  DT401.5.N58 2000
  976.73—dc21   99-36772
                                                                      CIP

Copyright © 2000 by Lucent Books, Inc.
P.O. Box 289011, San Diego, CA 92198-9011
Printed in the U.S.A.

CONTENTS

INTRODUCTION
A LAND OF MANY CONTRADICTIONS

From the time the first Europeans set foot on what is today modern Somalia, the land and the people have been a source of fascination. In 1854 when British explorer Richard Burton planned his pioneering expedition into Somalia, not much was known about that part of Africa. There were, however, many vague reports about the untold riches of the land and the hostile nature of the people. Col. James Outram, a British political agent in the nearby British colony of Aden, trying to dissuade Burton and other Europeans from traveling to Somalia, wrote that "the country was so extremely dangerous for any foreigners to travel in and the Somalis were of such a wild and inhospitable nature that no stranger could possibly live amongst them."[1] The hostile reports about the Somalis did not discourage Burton, an adventurer by nature, from making the journey. What he discovered during his travels was a people with a rich cultural heritage and a complex relationship to their land and to each other.

Somalia is a land of many contradictions. Many people have puzzled over the ironies the land and its people present. Scholars note that although the land is bordered by the Gulf of Aden to the north and the Indian Ocean to the east and south, much of Somalia is desert. Large portions of the country contain nothing but miles upon miles of sand and dried brush. Its desert environment means that the land can support only a small population. Most Somalis are pastoral nomads, a dangerous and difficult way of life, but the most suitable for their harsh environment. The nomads herd livestock—camels, goats, sheep, and cattle—and are constantly on the move in search of water and pasture. Most of the time, their arduous work yields just enough food to prevent them from starving. Starvation is never far from the mind and life of a Somali nomad. As one Somali proverb puts it, "Abundance and scarcity are never far apart; the rich and the poor frequent the same houses."

Yet, as many scholars have been quick to remark, even though the land fails to provide economically for the Somali people, it provides abundant nourishment for their imagination. Anthropologists Angela Fisher and Carol Beckwith point out that it is one of the great ironies of Somali life that the Somalis, who are forced by their dry land to live a difficult, pragmatic life as pastoral nomads, should find pleasure in composing and reciting stories and poetry. The Somalis are known throughout Africa for their uncommon gift for storytelling and poetry. Explorer Richard Burton was particularly impressed by this feature of Somali life, as he records in his travel descriptions:

> There are thousands of songs, some local, others general, upon all conceivable subjects, such as camel loading, drawing water, and elephant hunting; every man of education knows a variety of them. . . . The country

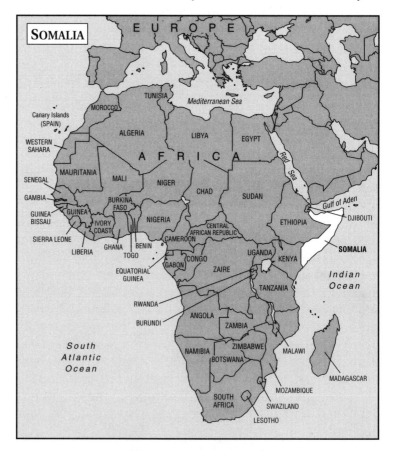

teems with "poets, poetasters, poetitos, poetaccios": [E]very man has his recognized position in literature as accurately defined as though he had been reviewed in a century of magazines—the fine ear of this people causes them to take the greatest pleasure in harmonious sounds and poetical expressions.[2]

The Somali people's love for poetry comes from, not in spite of, their relationship to their desert land. As they wander through the expanse of their barren land, the Somali people enjoy the sense of freedom their nomadic way of life gives them. The land, despite its aridity, is scenic and beautiful. The majestic mountains, the rolling plains, and the vastness of the sky under which the nomad sleeps inspire and nurture a poetic strain in a people forced to interact intimately with the natural world on a daily basis. The Somali poem "Fortitude" describes the Somalis' relationship to their land and way of life through its gracious rhythm and powerful imagery:

Explorer Richard Burton (shown here on a pilgrimage to the Muslim holy city of Mecca) was impressed with the Somalian poetry and storytelling.

> Like a she-camel with a large bell
> Come from the plateau and upper Haud,
> My heat is great. . . .
> One of my she-camels falls on the road
> And I protect its meat,
> At night I cannot sleep,
> And in the daytime I can find no shade.
> I have broken my nose on a stick,
> I have broken my right hip,
> I have something in my eye,
> And yet I go on.[3]

The paradoxes presented by the landscape and the Somali people's relationship to it parallel the contradictions existing in Somali social and political life. For example, Somali people speak the same language, share one religion, and trace their origin to a common ancestor. Having a common heritage has instilled in the Somalis a sense of pride in their country and their heritage. Unfortunately, this pride has not been enough to bring peace to Somalia.

A PEOPLE UNITED AND DIVIDED BY BLOOD

The Somalis are deeply divided among various clans who wage bitter wars against each other. It is like having different segments of one large family, each with deep, irreconcilable distrust and hatred for the other.

Interclan wars on the national level only underline divisions and conflicts on the local level. Within the clan, long-lasting feuds frequently end up in bloody wars. The main source of discord within the varous clans, scholars point out, is the profound Somali individualism and resilience. Though these qualities sustained them in a harsh environment for centuries, they also create fear and distrust of any centralized authority. Historically, clan members would come together to defend their clan when threatened by another clan. But in times of relative peace, members live separate lives, enjoying and defending their personal autonomy, sometimes even in opposition to other members of their own clan.

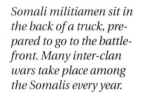

Somali militiamen sit in the back of a truck, prepared to go to the battle-front. Many inter-clan wars take place among the Somalis every year.

Fighting to assert oneself or to protect personal freedom becomes a way of life. As one Somali puts it, "When the clan is threatened by an outside force, we come together and defend the clan. When the enemy is defeated, we turn around and kill each other."[4]

Contact with the outside world has not lessened the many contradictions in Somali life. It has only made the problem worse. When France, Britain, and Italy colonized Somalia during the late nineteenth and early twentieth centuries, they used the internal differences among the Somalis in order to exploit the people's meager economic resources. When the European colonizers left the country in 1960, it could hardly be expected that the internal conflicts which had so deepened during colonial rule would disappear. With their characteristic belief in individual freedom, different segments of the population had different ideas on how best to rule the new country. The result was an unstable political environment that finally led to the Somali Civil War of the late 1980s and early 1990s. The Somali-born scholar Said Samatar describes the social and political conflict in Somalia most effectively when he says, "Where all are equal, anarchy is not far to seek."[5]

The civil war left Somalia in shambles. It is simply a jungle, say most observers of the Somali scene. The country has no recognizable political, social, or economic structures. Anarchy is reinforced as people continue to operate on the basis of each man for himself. There are no laws, no courts, no taxes, no social services, no trash collection, no public schools, no post office, no official currency, no means to settle defaulted business contracts, no public health system, and no police. Many scholars ask whether Somalia will find itself consumed by its own problems or unravel itself from the chaos that surrounds it and forge a new and strong nation as it enters the twenty-first century.

1

GEOGRAPHY

The Somali Democratic Republic is located in the northeastern corner of Africa, in a region known as the Horn of Africa. On the map, Somalia looks like an elongated number seven. To its north, separating it from the Arabian Peninsula, lies the Gulf of Aden. Its northwest is bordered by the nation of Djibouti. Ethiopia lies to its west and Kenya lies to the southwest. The Indian Ocean borders the eastern and southern portions of the country.

A nation just a little smaller than the state of Texas, Somalia is divided into three geographical zones: the northern region with its high mountains and plateaus; the southern region with low-lying plains and valleys; and the coastal region.

THE NORTHERN REGION

Northern Somalia is dominated by highlands and rugged mountain ranges and is occupied by pastoral nomads whose lives consist of moving with their sheep, goats, cattle, and camels across the mountainous terrain in search of water and pasture. The nomads divide the northern region into three zones—the Guban, the Kar Kar and Ogo Mountains, and the Haud.

THE GUBAN

Lying parallel to the Gulf of Aden, at the tip of the northern region, is a maritime plain called the Guban. Guban in the Somali language means scrub or burnt land. As its name suggests, the Guban is very dry and drab. Annual rainfall is about three inches, and this is concentrated during the monsoon season in the months of October to December. In the hot months between June and September, the Guban fully lives up to its name. Except for the urban populations at the ports of Berbera (population 150,000) and Zeila (population 60,000), the Guban is generally deserted during the dry months, when people in search of a cooler and greener climate retreat to the hills that rise to the south. Several shallow watercourses cut across the Guban, but they remain dry during most of the year, except for the rainy season. When the rains arrive, vegetation, which consists mostly of low bushes and grass clumps, is quickly renewed, and for a time the Guban provides grazing for the nomads' livestock. However, due to arid conditions, only desert plants like euphorbs and acacia grow in this area of the north during most of the year.

THE KAR KAR AND OGO MOUNTAINS

Inland from the Guban are the rugged ranges of the Kar Kar and Ogo Mountains. The Ogo and Kar Kar Mountains extend majestically from the northwestern border with Ethiopia to the tip of the Horn. The mountains descend in a series of sharp ledges to form a long, broad valley in the east known as the Nugaal Valley. The Nugaal contains an extended network of watercourses and wells and is thus home to large populations of nomads. But the low annual rainfall and the large population combine with frequent droughts to make life in the Nugaal hard.

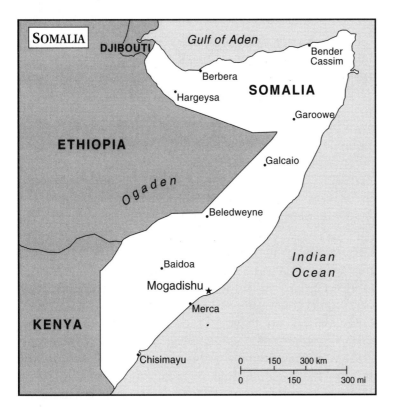

The vast majority of vegetation in the Guban consists of euphorbs and other desert plants.

Unlike the dry, drought-prone Nugaal Valley, the western part of the Ogo is the most pleasant and productive part of the north. This region is home to Somalia's third largest city, Hargeysa, with a population of seventy thousand. With an annual rainfall of about twenty inches, it is possible to cultivate crops like millet and corn in the region. The western part of the area contains water basins and permanent wells that provide a haven for nomads during the dry winter months. The town of Hargeysa is thus very crowded and busy during the dry times of the year. However, when the rainy season arrives, the nomads soon scatter into the surrounding regions.

THE HAUD

The highlands of the Ogo descend from Hargeysa toward the south to create the third northern zone, a broad, rolling wilderness known as the Haud. The Haud, which in northern Somali dialect simply means "south," provides the most extensive grazing land in Somalia and extends from the central to the western part of the country. The Haud also continues for more than one hundred miles into the Ogaden region of Ethiopia. The land is crossed by numerous valleys and natural depressions that form temporary lakes and ponds during the rainy seasons. Vegetation consists mainly of scattered acacia woodlands, tall grass, and interspersed belts of thick scrub. The rich grass provides excellent pasture for livestock. Because of its value, the Haud has been a point of contention between Ethiopia and Somalia since 1897, when the colonial powers established an international boundary between the two countries. Although the Haud was officially awarded to Ethiopia by the British in 1955, Somalia still claims sovereignty over the region.

THE SOUTHERN REGION

From the Haud, the Somali terrain descends gradually toward the southeastern coast, along the Indian Ocean, creating the low plains and valleys of the southern region. Rainfall is greater here than in the north. Just as significantly, the region contains the country's only two rivers, the Jubba and the Shabeelle. The rivers originate in the Ethiopian highlands to the north and descend southward, cutting wide valleys in the Somali plateau as they flow toward the Indian Ocean. The Jubba River enters the Indian Ocean at Chisimayu. The

The Haud provides extensive grazing land for livestock.

Shabeelle turns southwest near the town of Brava, about twenty miles north of Mogadishu, and follows a path parallel to the coast for about 140 miles. There it is finally lost in swampy, dry lands east of the town of Gelib. During the rainy season, the Shabeelle sometimes makes its way to the Jubba and from there to the sea.

In comparison to the north, the southern region of Somalia is relatively well watered. Annual rainfall is greater, about twenty inches, and the two rivers keep the land between them fertile for productive agriculture. Vegetation features open woodlands, mangrove forests, and rich pasturage. Even though some nomads live in the region, especially during the dry seasons, the south is mostly home to farmers, who grow a variety of crops, including millet, corn, cotton, rice, sugarcane, beans, peanuts, and citrus fruits. There are also a number of banana plantations in the area. As late as 1988, an average of a million tons of bananas were exported annually to other countries from the plantations in this region.

THE COASTAL TRADING CENTERS

Somalia has 1,880 miles of coastline, which is dotted with a number of cities and towns. The major coastal cities in the north are Zeila, Berbera, and Maydh. In the south are Mogadishu (Somalia's capital), Chisimayu, and Merca. Somalia's coastal cities have a distinguished history as centers of trade for the people of the Horn of Africa. Egyptian traders were visiting the Somali coast as early as 2000 B.C. In later centuries, merchants from the Arabian Peninsula, India, and China frequented these coastal cities. The Somalis exported such goods as incense, ivory, and gold in exchange for metals, textiles, cloves, and cinnamon.

Today, Somali coastal towns are still important economic centers. Each of the coastal towns has its own port. Unlike the small boats used for trading in early days, large ships carrying various types of goods now dock in Somalia. Mogadishu, Chisimayu, and Berbera have deepwater harbors protected by breakwaters, making these ports ideal for use by large cargo vessels. Mogadishu boasts the largest seaport in Somalia. This port is the one used by most international cargo ships. Berbera is the principal cargo port in the north and is used for the export of livestock. The port at Chisimayu is used for exporting goods produced primarily in the south,

such as bananas, cotton, sugarcane, and meat. Other ports at Maydh and Merca are smaller and are used for the export of small quantities of livestock and bananas, respectively.

The city of Mogadishu has the largest seaport in Somalia and is used by most international cargo ships.

Unlike the populations of Somalia's inland settlements, those of the coastal cities are diverse. Most foreigners living in Somalia—namely, Arabs, Asians, and Africans from other countries—establish themselves in the coastal towns. The mixture of these peoples gives Somali coastal towns a cosmopolitan atmosphere.

A PLACE OF EXTREMES

Somalia's proximity to the equator means that the climate is warm. Throughout the year, average temperatures range from 70 degrees Fahrenheit in the cooler months to about 108 degrees Fahrenheit in the hottest months. Temperatures in the mountains, however, can drop below zero in December and get as high as 125 degrees in July. The temperatures in the south, however, remain moderate at just over 80 degrees most of the year.

More than just the temperatures vary between extremes in Somalia. Rainfall is concentrated in the rainy seasons (April–June and October–December); the dry seasons are often harsh and droughts are frequent. Because of the scarcity of water, activities of the Somali nomads and farmers are structured around the seasons.

The Somalis recognize four major seasons: two dry *(jiilaal* and *hagaa)* and two rainy *(gu* and *dayr).* The cycle of the seasons is controlled by the northeast and southwest monsoons. The northeast wind is dry and dusty and brings drought; the southwest winds bring the rainy seasons.

The *jiilaal* is the first season of the year. It lasts from January to March and constitutes the winter season for the So-

---

PRAYER FOR RAIN

Droughts are a part of life in Somalia. Because of the frequency of droughts, the Somalis often perform rain-making ceremonies to ask God for rain. Poems in the form of prayers are usually constructed to commemorate such events. The prayer-poems acknowledge the power of God to do anything, including sending the much desired rain. This is a portion of a poem recited during a particularly severe drought in 1956:

> You who give sustenance to your creatures, O God,
> Put water for us in the nipples of rain!
> You who poured water into oceans, O God,
> Make this land of ours fertile again!
> Accepter of penance, who are wealthy, O God,
> Gather water in rivers whose beds have run dry!
> You who are steadfast and act justly, O God,
> Provide us with what we want you to grant!
> You who are glorious, truly bounteous, O God,
> Our cries have undone us, grant a shower of rain!
> You who are clement, truly worshiped, O God,
> Milk water for beasts which are stricken with thirst!
> Creator of nature who made all things, O God,
> Transmute our ruin to blessing and good!
> Eternal rewarder of merits, O God,
> Let that rain come which people used to drink!
> We have done much remembrance, O God who
>   remembers,
> Loosen upon us rain from the clouds!
> You who are merciful and compassionate, O God,
> Milk rain from the sky for Muslims in need!
> Giver of victuals at all times, O God,
> Who can do what you want, bestow on us rain!

malis. During this season the weather is hot, dry, and dusty. The *jiilaal* is the harshest of all the seasons for the Somali nomads. Many livestock die of thirst during this season. The lives of the nomads, who have to travel long distances in search of water and pasture for their animals, are often endangered. A Somali poem vividly describes Somalia during the dry season:

> Bush thick and impenetrable, scorched trees,
> the hot air rising from them,
> Hot wind and heat, which will lick you like flame . . .
> The swelling of feet pricked by thorns, a
> thorny thicket, plants prickly and spiny,
> Charred plants, hot stumps of burnt trees,
> the hot air rising from them. . . .[6]

In addition to the discomfort from the desert climate and the scarcity of resources, the nomads face constant hunger. With resources scarce during the *jiilaal,* the people manage to live just at subsistence level, with camel milk as their main diet.

The *jiilaal* is followed by the first rainy season, *gu.* The southwest monsoonal winds bring Somalia's heaviest rain. Life during the *gu* season, lasting from April to June, is the complete opposite of *jiilaal. Gu* is the season of plenty; rain falls, grass springs up and grows tall, livestock bring forth their young, milk is abundant, and food is relatively plentiful. Since water and pasture are in great supply, animals do not require much tending. The *gu* is the season when most local ceremonies such as marriages and religious coronations take place. Reprieved from four months of drought, people often come together to sing, dance, and recite poetry. As a rule, nomads and farmers regulate the breeding of livestock so that most of the young are born during or immediately after the *gu* season, when rich pasture is available to sustain life.

The *gu* season is followed by *hagaa* (July–September) with the return of the northeast monsoonal winds. By July, pastures in the north begin to dry up and dust raised by the strong winds is everywhere. The *hagaa* season is usually the hottest time of year, with temperatures reaching as high as 130 degrees Fahrenheit in the north. In the south, however, cooling breezes from the Indian Ocean make the season comparatively pleasant. *Hagaa* is the season of droughts and sandstorms in the north. Depending on the severity of the drought, the nomads may leave the higher plains for settlements in the valleys, where watering holes and wells can be found.

The last season of the year is the *dayr.* This is a brief rainy season which lasts from October to December and provides a period of relief from the *hagaa* drought and a chance to prepare for the harsh *jiilaal* season.

NATURAL RESOURCES

Because of its harsh desert climate, Somalia has very few trees. Forests or woodlands make up only about 14 percent of total land area. Some of the woodlands are located in the relatively wet regions of the northwest and the south. Aloes, euphorbs, acacias, and juniper are common in the higher elevations of the northwest; the south contains mangrove swamps. Boswellia and commiphora trees, from which frankincense and myrrh are made, grow in the drier lands of the northeast.

During the Hagaa season, large sandstorms whip across the northern lands of Somalia.

Although mining activities in Somalia have been very limited, the hilly lands and plateaus show good potential for the production of mineral resources. Currently, the main min-

eral resource is salt. Being bordered by the ocean makes salt production one of the most lucrative occupations in Somalia. Enough salt is produced for local consumption as well as for export.

A study conducted by the World Bank and the United Nations Development Program in 1992 indicates the presence of oil and gas in the hilly, uncultivable lands of the north. Limestone, gypsum anhydrite, uranium, and iron ore are present throughout the country. The region near the town of Hargeysa in the northwest is said to contain gold. But political instability and limited economic resources have prevented Somalia from tapping these resources. The country's inability to exploit its natural resources, combined with the harsh, arid climate, make life difficult for the Somalis. But since ancient times, they have learned to adapt to their environment, appreciate their land, and recognize the influence of natural elements on their way of life.

Thanks to its many miles of coastline, Somalia is able to create an industry based on its large supply of salt water. Salt remains the main mineral resource in Somalia today.

2

COLONIZATION

Somalia, as a nation, did not come into existence until July 1, 1960, when the northern and southern territories, including the coastal regions, were joined to form a single political entity. Before that time, Somalia consisted of a number of local enclaves ruled alternately by a clan head or an invading power. Because of its closeness to the Arabian Peninsula and its exposure to the sea, Somalia has attracted a host of outsiders, some with mercantile aims, but most with military conquest on their minds. At various points in its history, the Arabs, Portuguese, Italians, French, British, and Ethiopians all colonized or attempted to colonize the area now known as Somalia. Although the Somalis resisted foreign control and consciously strove to maintain their traditional institutions, these colonizing powers left their marks on the country's political and social institutions.

THE ARAB INFLUENCE

Somalia's position at the northeastern corner of Africa gives its coastal towns a unique opportunity to serve as centers of commerce for the Arabian Peninsula, Asia, and East and North Africa. For centuries, merchants have used the Somali coast as a meeting ground for the exchange of goods, such as frankincense, myrrh, ivory, skins and hides, livestock, textile materials, metal, tobacco, coffee, sugar, salt and other spices, and citrus fruits.

The constant trading relationship between the Somalis and their Arab neighbors led to a great influx of Arabs to the country during the seventh century A.D. Besides trade, the Arabs also brought their religion, which they spread with great fervor. By the thirteenth century, nearly all Somalis had converted to the Islamic faith, making Somalia one of the leading Muslim countries in Africa, with about 99 percent of the population practicing the faith. Following large-scale conversions to the Islamic religion, Somali coastal settlements—Zeila, Berbera, and Mogadishu in particular—already important centers of commerce, also emerged as

centers of Islamic culture and learning. Mosques and theological schools were built to teach Muslims about Islamic doctrines and values. The coastal towns were ruled by Arab sultans whose primary duty was to maintain the commercial nature of the region, collect taxes, and protect the town from foreign invasion.

Today, Arab political domination has ended, but Somali culture still shows considerable influence from the Arab world. Most Somalis have a functional knowledge of the Arabic language; and, although Somalis fervently try to maintain the purity of their language, a large percentage of their words have Arabic origins. Somali art, local crafts, and architectural design in coastal towns all show a clear Arab influence. In addition, all Somali religious and some secular festivals reveal Arab influence.

An open-air market in Mogadishu. For centuries merchants have used the Somali coast as a place to exchange spices, salt, tobacco, ivory, skins and hides, and other goods.

Buildings such as the Mosque of Sheik Abdulaziz, the oldest standing mosque in Somalia, show the influence that Arabs had on the country.

EUROPEAN COLONIZATION

Arab influence is a vital aspect of Somali cultural heritage, especially in relationship to their Islamic faith and cultural artifacts. However, Arab rule over Somalia began to weaken in the sixteenth century, when a group of Portuguese explorers bound for India got lost and landed at the Somali coastal town of Brava. A successful military campaign by the Portuguese against the ruling sultans of the eastern Somali coast followed. For a while the Portuguese ruled all Somali towns and their surrounding vicinities, with the sole exception of Mogadishu. The deposed sultans eventually regrouped and forced the Portuguese out of Somalia by 1728. But the Portuguese invasion marked the beginning of European colonization of Somalia.

By 1888, Somali territory had been effectively partitioned among three competing European colonial powers: Britain, Italy, and France. The British occupied northern and southeastern Somalia while the French occupied the northwest region. The Italians took the region in the south to northeast, which extended through the Nugaal Valley to the Bari region. The colonial powers all had different goals in establishing their presence in the region. However, they all shared economic motives as the basis for their imperial activities.

FRENCH SOMALILAND

The French colonization of Somalia began in 1862 when a treaty with the sultan of Obock placed that town under French control. In 1885 treaties with the sultans of Tadjoura, Gobaad, Ambado, and Djibouti extended French control throughout northwestern Somalia. The French wanted the territory for two reasons: first, they needed a coaling station on the East African coast for French ships traveling through the Red Sea and the Gulf of Aden to India; second, the French feared that if they did not annex northwest Somalia that the Italians or the British would.

France established its administrative center at Djibouti and began working to transform the desert town into a commercial center. Toward this goal, in 1899, a treaty with the Ethiopian emperor Menelik II allowed for the construction of a railroad to link Djibouti to the Ethiopian capital of Addis Ababa. Work on the railroad was completed in 1917. The easy access from Ethiopia to Djibouti allowed trade to flourish between the two countries.

For the most part, French rule in northwestern Somalia was peaceful and seemed to have the support of the people. But the creation of French Somaliland effectively established an international boundary in northwest Somalia that split the Somali people between two different administrations—

THE NORTHERN FRONTIER PROVINCE

The history of British activities in the Northern Frontier Province is similar to that of the Ogaden region. At the turn of the century, the British colonial territories in the Horn included northern Somalia and the region known as the Northern Frontier Province. The Northern Frontier Province is a vast desert land that covers about forty-five thousand square miles along the boundary between Somalia and Kenya. The region is almost completely inhabited by Somali nomads of the Ogaden and Hawiye clans. The nomads who live in the area wandered freely across the region tending to their animals.

After the British created a province and established a military presence in the region, questions were constantly raised as to whether the land belonged to Somalia or Kenya. Somalia claims the region as part of its land since it is occupied by Somalis. The Kenyans, on the other hand, argue that historically the land belongs to them. They claim that Somali nomads only settled the land during their southward expansion in the sixteenth century, resulting in the dispossession of the original Kenyan inhabitants. After much debate and to the dismay of the Somalis, the land was officially given by Britain to Kenya in 1963, when Kenya gained its independence. Kenya and Somalia still fight over the region. But Kenyans are not eager to give up what constitutes a fifth of their land, even though it is primarily inhabited by people who are ethnically Somali.

French rule for those living in the northwest as far as Djibouti and British rule for those living on the other side of the border, from Zeila to north-central Somalia.

BRITISH SOMALILAND

At the same time that France was negotiating treaties and building up its territory in French Somaliland, the British were at work in northern and southeast Somalia. Southeast Somalia, the region now known as the Northern Frontier District of Kenya, was used as a military outpost to oversee the British colonial activities in Kenya. Northern Somalia, on the other hand, was acquired by the British for purely economic reasons. By 1830, Britain, an established colonial power, had colonized India and was benefiting from trade with that country. In order to safeguard the passage of its ships from India through the Gulf of Aden and into the Red Sea, Britain conquered Aden, located on the southern tip of the Arabian Peninsula, only about 120 miles from the coast of northern Somalia.

A British officer leads a patrol from the Somaliland Camel Corps along the border of British Somaliland in 1936. Britain established itself in the north and southeast parts of the country in the 1800s.

SAYYID MUHAMMAD IBN ABD ALLAH HASAN

During the height of British and Italian colonization of Somalia, one of the people who rose to challenge imperial control was a Somali by the name of Sayyid Muhammad ibn 'Abd Allah Hasan. Hasan was a religious leader and a warrior from the Ogaden clan. He was also a poet. These three attributes made him a formidable opponent of imperialism. Hasan understood the power of Somali language and poetry in mobilizing the people to action. He used his poetry to speak out on what it meant to be a Somali and the disgrace of having foreign powers rule Somalia. Hasan was so outspoken in his criticism of colonial activities in Somalia that the British nicknamed him the "Mad Mullah of Somalia."

With his followers, Hasan led a twenty-one-year guerrilla war against the British, Italian, and Ethiopian colonists in Somalia. His primary message was that if the imperialists continued to stay in Somalia, they would face constant opposition and war. In poem after poem, he argued that Somalia had nothing to offer colonial powers. The Somali people should be left in peace. Hasan died on November 23, 1920, at the age of fifty-six. He died forty years before Somalia was granted independence. Today, he is considered a Somali national hero.

The annexation of Aden gave the British the invaluable strategic position it needed to dominate the trade route through the Red Sea. It provided a good harbor for British ships, and British soldiers were stationed there to keep control over sea activities. But Aden was sparse in resources. Somalia, not far from Aden, proved to be the source of the provisions that the British needed to maintain their garrison in Aden.

In 1885, Britain, after much negotiation and military intimidation, signed a treaty with the sultans of Berbera and surrounding towns. In this way northern Somalia became an official territory of Britain. By 1888, the British territory (known as the British Protectorate of Somaliland) had extended inland, covering northern to central Somalia.

Since Britain's interest in Somalia was mainly economic, colonial officials did not interfere with the lives of the Somali people. While at first glance this policy of non-interference in the affairs of the Somalis might seem to have benefited them, it did not. In essence the policy meant that the colonial rulers took from the Somalis what the British needed without giving anything in return. The British neglect of its Somali protectorate ensured that the culture of the people remained intact. But it also meant that the nation would have no economic infrastructure to rely on when the colonial regime ended.

ITALIAN SOMALILAND

Much like Britain, Italy saw Somalia as a territory that would offer it economic opportunities. The presence of the Jubba and the Shabeelle Rivers in the region suggested to the Italians that the land would be suitable for cultivating crops, especially coffee.

Unfortunately for Italy, southern Somalia did not yield the hoped-for riches. The land turned out to be less fertile than the colonists had hoped; moreover, the Somalis, who resented foreign occupation of their land, refused to work on the plantations the Italians had established. The lack of Somali cooperation and sparse land productivity frustrated the Italians. If its economic goals were to be achieved, Italy needed to acquire more land. With this in mind, Italy invaded first Ethiopia and then British Somaliland.

SOMALILAND DURING WORLD WAR II

Although Italy successfully conquered both countries, the occupation proved short-lived. In January 1941, British forces, from their base in the Northern Frontier District, reinforced with troops from India and South Africa, launched a counterattack. The British not only recovered their territory from the Italians, but led a military campaign that forced Italians out of southern Somaliland and Ethiopia as well. The defeat of Italian forces was not only humiliating for Italy, it also meant that, as of 1941, Italy no longer controlled any territory in Somalia. The greater part of Somalia was now under British rule.

THE TRUST TERRITORY

After forcing the Italians out of Ethiopia and southern Somalia, the question facing Britain was what to do with Somalia. Britain wanted to continue its presence in northern Somalia as well as the Ogaden region, but southern Somaliland constituted a problem. Britain was not interested in taking on the responsibilities and the expenses of running the region; understandably, it did not want to give southern Somaliland back to Italy.

By the late 1940s, a decision needed to be reached about the fate of Somalia. Britain, at the suggestion of its foreign secretary, Ernest Bevin, proposed that all three territories be administered by Britain but given the status of a United Nations trust territory. This meant that the Somalis would have a great share in running their country. Since complete independence was not an option, Somali leaders favored the British proposal. Italy, of course, opposed the plan. After much negotiation, it

 GREATER SOMALIA

By the late 1940s, educated Somalis were not only asking for independence from their colonial rulers, but arguing for the need for the Somali people to be united under one nation. One of the leading political parties during the period, the Somali Youth League, led by Haji Muhammad Hussein, submitted a memorandum to the commission established by the United Nations to find out the will of the people. The memorandum read:

> We wish our country to be amalgamated with other Somalilands and to form one political, administrative and economic unit with them. We Somalis are one in every way. We are the same racially and geographically, we have the same culture, we have the same language, and the same religion. There is no future for us except as part of a greater Somalia. The present International frontiers are artificial and the divisions are placing unfair strain on the political, administrative, and economic welfare of the country. The existence of several foreign official languages with the several territories, is enough, in itself to make aliens out of brothers of the same race, religion, country, and put back our national advancement indefinitely. . . . We want it [unity] and the Somalis of other territories also want it. By this union only can we have opportunity to give full expression to our national spirit and work out our destiny as a nation of normal human beings. Union with other Somalilands is our greatest demand which must take priority over all other considerations.

A group of Moslem judges sits and listens to campaign speeches given in October 1958 during municipal elections. Although under foreign rule at the time, Somalis had at least some say in their government.

was agreed that southern Somaliland, the former Italian Somaliland, would be placed under a United Nations trust under Italian jurisdiction, with independence to be granted to the Somalis within ten years. The Ogaden region and British Somaliland would remain under British control.

In retrospect, scholars argue that this was the first missed opportunity for the unification of the greater part of Somalia. In 1949, Britain ceded part of the Ogaden territory back to Ethiopia; the rest, including the Haud, was returned in 1955, thus effectively placing the Somalis living in the region again under Ethiopian sovereignty.

TOWARD INDEPENDENCE

In both British and Italian Somaliland, 1950 to 1960 was a period of preparing the Somali people for independence. To make up for the neglect of previous decades, the Italian government committed itself to establishing schools to provide Somalis with the basic skills needed for self-rule. Elementary and secondary schools were opened, and many Somali students from the south enrolled. The language of instruction in the schools was Italian. Although the Italian effort at providing infrastructure and formal education for the local Somalis was inadequate, it was instrumental in creating a cadre of Somali elite who would eventually assume control of the government.

In another move designed to prepare Italian Somaliland for independence, a Somali-based advisory council, known as the Territorial Council, was established in 1950. This was the first time that Somali nationals had been permitted to occupy legislative positions in the Italian-administered

Somali students carry banners through the streets of Mogadishu in honor of the nation's independence on July 1, 1960.

territory. Territory-wide elections were held in 1954 and in 1959 to elect members to the council. Both the 1954 and 1959 elections established a democratic precedent for the emerging Somali nation to follow.

In British Somaliland, meanwhile, transition to self-government moved at a slower pace. The first election was not held until February 17, 1960, with universal adult male

THE ETHIOPIAN-SOMALI CONFLICT

The relationship between Somalia and Ethiopia has not always been hostile. In fact, until the nineteenth century relations were cooperative and friendly. Nomads from both countries moved freely across the border in search of water and land for grazing. The conflict between Ethiopia and Somalia comes primarily from their disagreement over the Ogaden region, which Britain gave Ethiopia under terms of the 1897 Anglo-Ethiopian agreement, even though it was occupied primarily by Somalis. In modern times, even though many Ethiopians do not consider the Ogaden as part of Ethiopia, the Ethiopian government has insisted on retaining possession of the region. As Saadia Touval explains in his book, *Somali Nationalism*:

> Unlike the Somalis who constitute one ethnic group, the population of Ethiopia is a conglomeration of several ethnic groups with different cultures, and religions, and speaking about fifty different languages. Each of these groups making up Ethiopia has at one time or the other sought independence from Ethiopia. Returning the Ogaden region to Somalia would constitute a major risk for Ethiopia. At stake for Ethiopia would be not only one-fifth of its territory, but the very foundations of its state. If the principle of secession is conceded to the Somalis, it may stimulate demands by other sections of the population and gravely threaten the continued existence of the Ethiopian state in its present form. Ethiopia and Somalia have fought two wars over the region. The first was in 1963, shortly after northern and southern Somalia gained their independence. The latest was the 1978 Ogaden War, orchestrated by Siad Barre's military regime. Somalia lost both wars.

suffrage. Thirty-three Somalis were elected to the Legislative Assembly and four were elected to administrative positions. The pace of independence moved much faster after the elections. On April 6, the newly elected Legislature adopted a motion calling for independence and union with the southern territory as soon as it became independent on July 1, 1960.

With a growing demand for independence, Britain felt it was much better to have Somalis as friends than enemies in the region. On June 26, 1960, barely four months after northern Somali leaders were elected into administrative positions, Britain ceded its control over northern Somaliland. Four days later, on June 30, 1960, the Italian trust over southern Somalia ended, and Italian Somaliland regained its independence on July 1, 1960. The same day, the Legislative Assemblies of both territories met and agreed to merge into a single unit. The Somali nation was born, under the name of the Democratic Republic of Somalia.

The Somalis were happy to have their independence. The poem "Independence," written to celebrate the occasion, gives thanks to God for the people's freedom from colonial rule, emphasizing the religious nature of the Somali worldview:

> Freedom and dignity have reached us,
> We have brought together the two lands.
> Glory to God!
> Say: "It is God's victory,
> It is God's victory!
> We are victorious.
> Beat the song, join the dance!
> Everyone, with all your might!
> And now let us finish, cease!
> It is God's victory!
> It is God's victory![7]

THOSE LEFT BEHIND

Detracting from the independence celebration, however, was the knowledge that a third of the Somali people were still under the administration of other colonial powers—the Ogaden territory, which the British ceded to Emperor Haile Selassie of Ethiopia in 1955; the Northern Frontier District, still under British control; and French Somaliland, still under French rule.

In 1970, the French left French Somaliland, but neither the land nor the people were returned to Somalia. That territory formed its own nation under the name of Djibouti, with half of its population consisting of ethnic Somalis. Britain, meanwhile, ceded the Northern Frontier Province to Kenya in 1963. The nationalist Somalis, whose effort had helped gain independence for northern and southern Somaliland, had vowed to fight to reunify their people. The promise is still yet to be fulfilled.

THE PEOPLE AND THEIR SOCIETY

Culturally, Somalis are one people who share a common lineage, faith, and language. Although the Somali people probably came originally from Ethiopia, they owe many aspects of their culture to Arabs who migrated in the seventh century to what is now Somalia.

Over a span of some three hundred years, these Arabs settled among the Somalis, bringing with them their Islamic faith. By the thirteenth century A.D., the Somalis had almost completely converted to Islam; today, 99 percent of Somalis are practicing Muslims.

THE ISLAMIC RELIGION

Like Muslims everywhere, Somalis are required to observe the five pillars of the faith: a firm belief that there is only one God (in Arabic, Allah), and that Muhammad is his prophet; praying five times a day, facing the direction of the holy city of Mecca; giving alms to the poor or those less fortunate; observing the month of Ramadan through fasting; and undertaking a pilgrimage to Mecca at least once during a person's lifetime, if possible.

The Somali day begins with the rhythmic but piercing cry of the muezzin calling the faithful to their morning prayers. Traditionally, the muezzin would climb the tower of the mosque and recite the rhythmic chants loudly enough to be heard throughout the city or village, waking the people to their first duty of the day—praying. These days, the call is usually broadcast over loudspeakers. When the muezzin calls believers to prayer in the morning, several times he sings the words *"Allahu akbar,"* which mean "God is great."

THE SOMALI CLANS

Even more than adherence to a single religion, Somalis look to their clan membership for identity. Because they see

37

For Muslims, prayer is an important part of daily life. Here Somali Muslims kneel in prayer facing the holy city of Mecca.

themselves as descendants of one mythical father, the Somalis form one ethnic group. As one Somali puts it, "we are one people, all brothers and sisters."[8] Belonging to one ethnic group, however, has not been enough to hold the Somalis together. They are deeply divided by clan. Although the various clans are related, they are often hostile to one another.

The Somalis maintain their sense of belonging and identity through tracing their distinct family origins. One scholar of Somali life, I. M. Lewis, notes the relative ease with which Somali children as young as six or seven years old can recite their genealogical lines up to twenty generations. It is the mother's responsibility to teach her children about their heritage, and the teaching begins in the cradle. David D. Laitin, a Canadian who lived and worked in Somalia for many years, says that most Somalis ask a stranger about his or her lineage line. Knowing another's lineage is important because, for the most part, it determines whether one should consider the person a friend or an enemy. Most internal wars in Somalia are fought among different clans, so ultimately a person's security depends on the strength and goodwill of fellow clan members.

The Somali clan system operates on four different levels. In descending order of size, the four levels are: the genealogical family, the clan family, the primary lineage group, and the *diya*-paying unit. At the top of the genealogical tree are the two ancestral families, representing the two original forefathers to whom all Somalis trace their beginning—Saab and Samaale. The Saab family contains two clans—the Digil and the Rahanwin—who occupy the southern part of the country between the Jubba and the Shabeelle Rivers. They are mainly farmers and comprise about 25 percent of the Somali population. The Samaale family group contains four clans—the Isaaq, Hawiye, Dir, and Darood. Members of these clans are primarily pastoral nomads and therefore are distributed throughout the country, although the Isaaq and the Dir clans live mainly in the north. The Hawiye clan occupies the southern region with the Digil and Rahanwin. The Darood clan is evenly distributed through the north and the south.

A Somali mother and daughter laugh together. It is the responsibility of Somali mothers to teach their children about their heritage.

Each clan numbers between twenty thousand to 2 million people, meaning that a clan is usually too large and its members too dispersed to act cooperatively as a single social or political group. Collective actions are mostly carried out through the primary lineage groups that are subsidiaries of the clans.

Each of the six clans are divided into subgroups known as the primary lineages. In simple terms, a primary lineage can be considered a large extended family consisting of members who can trace their common ancestry from six to ten named generations. A Somali's sense of identity and allegiance belongs to his or her primary lineage; and, although it is not considered incestuous to do so, people are still forbidden to marry others within the same primary lineage. Marriages take place between people of different primary lineages.

THE *DIYA*-PAYING GROUP

The *diya*-paying group functions as the primary political and social unit in Somalia. As Christian P. Potholm states in his book, *Four African Political Systems:*

In a society where genealogy determines the place of individuals, the *diya*-paying groups form an avenue by which Somali males form associations with others based on interests and fluid social contracts. Depending on location and ecological situations, such as the availability of water and land for grazing, the *diya*-paying group may range in size from 120 to 9,000 persons. The *diya*-paying groups were originally fighting units of Somali males, consisting of "close kinsmen united by a specific contractual alliance whose terms stipulate that they should pay and receive blood compensation in consort." Blood compensation is based on the stipulations of Islamic law as applied by the Somali. There are three specific types of offences: *dil* (homicide), *goon* (wounding), and *dalliil* (loss of face or damages). In the harsh struggle for life in the Horn of Africa, where the margin of survival was seldom wide and every able-bodied man was needed, the Somalis tended to use compensation of camels and other livestock wherever possible. Joining a band to reduce one's liability was essential. By accepting a common share of the fortunes of a *diya*-paying group, an individual would no longer stand alone, he would have protection, status, and a place in the society. The process of identification with one's *diya*-paying group is centuries old and has not died out with the thrust of modernity, for the *diya*-paying group represents the primary building block of Somali politics.

DIYA-PAYING GROUPS

Since it is often impossible for all members of an extended family, especially one as large as a Somali lineage group, to agree with one another, Somali society is further divided into smaller political units known as *diya*-paying groups, or *heer*.

The *heer* is the basic traditional political institution in Somalia. Membership is based on paying a certain fee and agreeing to abide by the social contract, which is drawn up by members for the purpose of defending their interests against those of other groups. Members of a *heer* are often from the same lineage, traceable up to eight generations, and may number from 250 to 3,000 men and women. Decisions affecting members of the group are made in consultation with all adult male members of the community. Women are not allowed to take part in public decision making.

"Diya" is an Arabic word meaning "blood wealth." The essential duty of the *diya*-paying groups is to pay and receive compensation for actions committed by or against members of their group, especially in issues relating to injuries and death. If one member of a *diya*-paying group is injured or killed by another group, or if his property is attacked, the wronged group is pledged to collective vengeance, or, if reparation is made, to sharing the compensation paid among all its male members.

When a decision needs to be made, male members of the *heer* assemble; and, sitting face-to-face, they deliberate on the issue at hand. Every male over the age of fifteen is considered worthy of political participation and allowed to speak at such a general assembly *(shir)*. The meetings are presided over by a council of elders. The council of elders, however, has no power over the people. As David D. Laitin and Said S. Samatar indicate, *"shir* assemblies are often dominated by men with wealth, skill in public oratory or poetry, religious knowledge or bravery. But the high status that derives from wealth or skills confers no special rights or privileges."[9] Decisions are still reached through a democratic process. The elders would never take any action which lacks the support of the majority of the people.

Conflicts between members of the community are decided by the council of elders in accordance with Islamic law *(sharia)* and Somali traditions. The responsibility of the elders includes interpreting Islamic as well as customary regulations. The council follows a strict procedure that involves the plaintiffs laying out his case before the court, including calling witnesses, if he so chooses. Then the accused is given an opportunity to refute or accept the charge. If the charge is refuted by the accused, the council then deliberates on the merits of the case. Cases brought before the court often involve civil issues such as marriage, divorce, family disputes, inheritance, land tenure, water and grazing rights, injuries, property damage, and payment of *diya* or blood compensation.

AN EGALITARIAN SOCIETY

Almost everyone who visits Somalia comments on the egalitarian nature among males of its traditional political structure. Every Somali male is expected to participate in political decision making. David Laitin, an anthropologist who lived and worked in Somalia for many years, narrates an experience that supports this view. He says:

> When I was teaching at the National Teacher Education Center in 1969, I attended daily meetings of my departmental staff to talk over issues concerning curriculum and individual student and teacher problems. It took me a long time to accept the fact that the school's bus driver and cook could come into our meetings, sit down, and actually participate. To the Somalis this did not seem strange, and I watched once, incredulously, as the bus driver discussed an educational issue. To the Somalis, our meeting was not unlike the *shir,* where all adult males of the political community (the *heer*) are legitimate participants. His participation demonstrated as well the lack of authority roles in Somali society; in no realm are certain people more legitimate spokesmen than others. This is reflected in the Somali language where there are few honorific titles and no words for "Mr.," "Mrs.," or "Sir." Everyone from the nomadic child to the president of the Republic is called by his first name, often by a childhood nickname, and a person's name is almost never preceded by a title.

MARRIAGE AND FAMILY

While the *heer* functions as the basic political unit in Somalia, the family forms the backbone of Somali society. Families are often large, since Somali men are allowed to have as many as four wives—the maximum permitted under Islamic law. Because the responsibility for caring for the children falls on the mother, bonds between children and their mothers tend to be stronger than bonds between children and their fathers. Moreover, while the ties between children of the same father are often strong, the ties between children of the same mother are stronger. In the ordinary course of daily life, men who share the same father normally associate with and support each other without distinction; but if they also have the same mother they tend to meet as well in the more intimate social life of the evening, discuss matters more freely, and help each other or even scheme together.

Somali mothers teach their children through example and folklore the values cherished by society. Children learn to respect their parents and elders and that they must not behave in such a manner as to bring disgrace to the family. One Somali, Ali Abdi, says that no matter how old one gets, one never forgets that one has a duty to show respect to one's parents and elders. He notes that his brother, who is forty-four years old and a family man with his own children, still obeys and listens to his parents. "Thinking about it, it is strange," he says. "But that's what's expected of us and we do it. We also expect our own children to obey and respect us as we obey and respect our own parents."[10]

Despite the tightly knit nature of Somali families, marriage is not viewed simply as a union between two people; it is a public affair that unites the families and lineages of the couple. Because of this, parents often arrange the marriages of their children. In selecting a bride or groom for their child, parents weigh many factors, including wealth and social standing of the family, character, physical strength, and the advantage of the union in the wider context of clan politics.

A Somali man stands with a group of children. Somali men may have many children by more than one wife.

For example, marriages have often been used to seal a peace agreement between two clans.

It is uncommon for a daughter or son to refuse to marry the person his or her parents have chosen. If one should refuse the arranged marriage, one may elope with the person of his or her choice, but such a move means cutting all ties with his or her family. A child may also wait until the parents find a marriage partner they do approve of.

THE MARRIAGE CONTRACT

When a match is made and the child agrees with the parents' choice, the groom's family formally initiates the marriage process. The oldest male member of the groom's family approaches the girl's family and asks for her hand in marriage. If the proposal is accepted, a small token of livestock or money is given to the bride's family to establish the engagement of the couple. In the following weeks, the bride-wealth, or *yarad,* is negotiated and paid. The groom's family pays bride-wealth, usually in the form of livestock, to the bride's

On a bride's wedding day, her mother and close friends demonstrate the duties she will be expected to perform in her household. These include sweeping the floor, grinding grain, and serving guests.

SOMALI WOMEN

Somali women play an important economic role in their society. These days, more and more women are receiving formal education and serving in various capacities in the public lives of their community. However, their place in society continues to be one of submission. As I. M. Lewis explains in his book *Saints and Somalis:*

> Whether as daughters or as wives, women are subject to strong and direct control by their menfolk. A man may, within limits that are only vaguely defined, beat an erring wife and can expect the support of her kin in any corrective action he takes as long as they are interested in the maintenance of the marriage. Indeed, the perfect image of the husband, as of the father, is the stern *pater familias* with full authority to compel obedience and submission. On his wedding night, according to tradition, the husband is expected to chastise his wife with a small ceremonial whip, the public display of which is a sign of his newly married position. These powers vested in men are firmly upheld by the Muslim legal courts, although a woman can, at least in theory, appeal against physical mistreatment. Husbands, moreover, can divorce their wives very easily, and in fact do, while women cannot directly gain a divorce and can only have their marriages annulled, on such grounds as the physical incapacity of their husband. They can of course resort to other remedies—such as simply absconding. But as long as the wife's kin are committed to the continuance of her marriage every effort will be made by them to find the run-away wife, and if caught, she will be beaten and returned to her husband.

family (the oldest male member of the bride's family receives the bride-wealth). In turn, the bride's family is expected to return a portion, not more than two-thirds, of the bride-wealth to the groom's family. For example, a groom's family may give twenty-eight camels and fifty sheep and goats as the bride-wealth. The bride's family may return as many as fifteen camels and household goods to the groom's family as an exchange gift. The returned gifts are called *dibaad* and usually become the property of the groom. The *dibaad,* therefore, provides the bride and groom with materials to begin their new household.

Once the bride-wealth has been paid and the *dibaad* received, the marriage ceremony can then take place. The Somali wedding ceremony is simple. It consists of the bride and groom appearing before a sheik (a Muslim religious leader) who blesses them and pronounces them man and wife. The groom seals the marriage by giving a small gift, the dower, to the bride.

While the wedding ceremony is simple, the marriage feast or celebration that follows is elaborate. The marriage feast, which is given by the bride's family, lasts for seven days. During the feast, the bride's family entertains the families and friends of the bride and groom with food, singing, and dancing. The wedding guests give small gifts to the bride and groom and wish them happiness and many children.

DIVORCE

Despite the elaborate nature of the Somali marriage process, the divorce rate in Somalia is relatively high. Current statistics estimate the figure at about 37 percent. Because Somalia is a male-oriented society, husbands can obtain a divorce from their wives easily. Under Islamic law, if a man wants to divorce his wife, all he needs to do is to tell her "I divorce you" three times. After that, the divorce is legally recognized in Somalia.

Women, on the other hand, cannot directly obtain a divorce. A woman who finds unbearable problems in her marriage can only have it annulled after many appeals to an Islamic court, and then only with the support of her birth family. If for some reason a woman's birth family refuses to go along with a divorce, the woman's only escape is to run away and make sure she is not found. If she is found, she will more than likely be brought back to her husband, who will likely abuse her even more.

However, if a family supports an annulment that is subsequently granted, the woman may not remarry within three months. This waiting period is imposed to make certain that the woman was not pregnant at the time of the divorce. In Somalia, a child always belongs to the father, even if the parents are divorced. After the waiting period, a woman is allowed to remarry and often does.

LANGUAGE

In addition to a common religion and a network of kinship ties, Somalis are linked by a common language. The Somali

HIDDEN MESSAGES

Somali linguistic skills more than serve an aesthetic purpose. Sometimes the language functions as a technique for hiding important information from outsiders. Oral messages can be sent long distances, with the bearer of the message remaining in complete ignorance of the true meaning of the message carried.

A popular story is told by many scholars to illustrate how allegorical diction (guudmar) is used to hide verbal messages from messengers. The story is about a young Sufi, or Islamic mystic, named Raage Ugaas. Although he came from a wealthy family, Raage renounced all worldly goods and joined an itinerant band living an ascetic existence. Since this group attempted to teach nomads the joys of restraint, they felt that they could not beg or even complain when they themselves suffered from thirst or hunger. One day Raage met a man who was going to his father's region and gave him the following message: "I am safe and I am learning things well and I am at such and such a stage in my studies. The members of the college are in good health. We are all right and are learning things well. I shall just say to you that for evening prayers I use the ablutions which I performed for the early morning prayers."

The messenger, who did not understand the intent of the message, duly delivered it to Raage's father. Raage's father, after some thought, did understand. Since one must perform ablutions before each of the five daily prayers if one passes water, feces, or wind since the last prayer, he figured that must have meant Raage was suffering from starvation. So when the messenger was preparing to return to Raage, Raage's father gave him a vessel of thirty pieces of dried meat and some ghee (clarified butter), with the following message: "Your father said that today the month has reached its thirtieth day and the water pond is full for us." When Raage received the container and the message, he saw that the vessel level was down to two hand spans and that there were only twenty-three pieces of meat, and so he asked the messenger for the remainder. The messenger was startled, but Raage explained to him that the thirtieth day referred to the number of pieces of meat and that the full pond referred to the full vessel.

language is intricately laced with imagery, allegories, and proverbs, all of which are part of everyday speech. The Somalis, says anthropologist David Laitin, value the spoken word in much the same way that they value the prowess of a warrior. To be recognized as a man of worth in society, the individual must have the reputation of being a fearless fighter as well as being skilled in the art of public speaking.

The Somali language and its traditions reflect and powerfully record the cultural heritage of the Somalis, the things that unite them and the things that divide them. Beyond that, it reminds observers of the complex culture of the Somali people, a culture steeped in history. It is a society that is both unified and divided by its heritage and as such continues to intrigue and baffle outsiders who seek to have a better understanding of the Somali people's way of life.

Somali Government and Politics: A Quest for Order

Since the first days of its independence, Somalia has been searching for political stability. For the first nine years of its life as an independent nation, Somalia had a democratically elected government that the international community hoped would serve as a model for other nations newly freed from their colonial rulers. But internal conflicts and a weak economy left the government unable to deal with the nation's problems. A military government that took over following a coup led by Maj. Gen. Muhammad Siad Barre in 1969, rather than solving the problems of the country, introduced dictatorial policies that intensified the conflicts and divisions among the Somalis. The result was a civil war, from 1988 to 1992, that completely destroyed the economic and political infrastructure of the country. Today, Somalia has no central government. Different parts of the country are controlled by different clan leaders or militia. As the Somali writer Nuruddin Farah states, "anarchy is the order of day."[11]

Parliamentary Democracy

The political system formed at the creation of the Somali state in 1960 was modeled after the governments of Somalia's colonizers. When independence came, the goal was to integrate the Italian and the British political legacies while respecting the Islamic laws that the Somali people had traditionally followed. There were three branches of government—the executive, the legislative, and the judiciary—designed to allow personal freedom and the right of the people to determine their own fate. Every Somali male over the age of eighteen had the right to vote.

At the national level, the people elected members of the National Assembly, who had the power to make the laws by

49

Major General Siad Barre turned the Somali court system into a puppet of the country's military government.

which all Somalis would abide. Members of the Assembly in turn elected the president of the republic, who would serve for a term of six years with a maximum of two terms. The president was the head of state and commander-in-chief of the armed forces. In addition to these duties, the president was responsible for appointing the prime minister from among members of the National Assembly. The responsibility of the prime minister and those he chose as members of his cabinet, fourteen in all, was to implement laws passed by the National Assembly.

At the local level, Somalia was divided into sixteen administrative regions under the control of a governor and a council elected by the people. The regions were further divided into eighty-four smaller districts ruled by popularly elected councils.

THE JUDICIARY

Like the legislative and executive branches of government, the Somali judiciary was modeled after those of the colonial powers. The 1961 Somali constitution provided for a four-tiered court system. The highest court of the land was the Supreme Court, followed in descending order by two appeals courts, eight regional courts, and eighty-four district courts.

Although Somalia's judiciary was structured like those of many European nations, one significant difference was that none of Somalia's courts made use of juries to decide cases. Instead, verdicts were determined by the judge and his assistants.

The Somali court system was designed to interpret the nation's constitution and see to it that the nation's laws were obeyed. For the first nine years of its existence, from 1960 to 1969, it was a model institution for upholding the rule of law. However, after the 1969 coup d'etat led by Maj. Gen. Muhammad Siad Barre, the court system, although not altered structurally, by and large became the puppet of the military administrations that arrested, convicted, and imprisoned political opponents without due process. Currently, with a decentralized government and continuing political instability, the court system is virtually nonfunctional.

THE 1969 COUP D'ETAT

By 1969, the Somali people were disenchanted with their elected government. Competition for power between members of the legislature from the north and the south meant

SCIENTIFIC SOCIALISM

When General Siad Barre seized power from the democratically elected government in October 1969, he adopted a system of government which he called "Scientific Socialism." As I. M. Lewis, one of the leading scholars of Somali history, reveals in his book *Blood and Bone: The Call of Kinship in Somali Society,* it was a system that went completely awry. Its end result was a civil war that completely destroyed the Somali state and the lives of its people. He states:

General Siad Barre adopted "Scientific Socialism" . . . with the stated aim of uniting the nation and eradicating its ancient clan divisions. "Tribalism," which was associated with nepotism and corruption, was officially banned and ritually buried (1971) and "tribalistic" (i.e., clan-based) behavior became a serious criminal offence. The collective payment of blood money was correspondingly outlawed and the personal rather than kinship aspects of marriage emphasized. The universal term of address "cousin"—implying clansman— was officially replaced by the term *jaalle*—comrade. Lineage genealogies, the traditional basis of socio-political identity, and their use to identify people were banned: even the old nationalistic circumlocution "ex-clan" was forbidden. In their place, the Head of State was presented in the revolutionary rhetoric as the "Father" of a nation whose "Mother" was his Revolution. This stirring ideology—legitimated by reference to Marx, Lenin, and Siad—was thrust upon the masses through intense radio propaganda and through the local Orientation Centers which were set up throughout the state, which had itself been divided into new provinces cutting across traditional clan boundaries. Radiating out from the presidency, the locally organized people's vigilantes (or "Victory Pioneers"—led by the "Victorious Leader" Siad), and the sinister National Security Service shared the task of ensuring that this elaborated propaganda rhetoric was to replace archaic, divisive lineage loyalty, by that little day-to-day administrative business was conducted. Many accused government officials of being corrupt, of practicing nepotism, and making decisions based on clan loyalty rather than the good of the nation. In an attempt to improve confidence in the government, a new election was called in March 1969. Despite wide participation in the March elections, the people's disgust with their government remained.

On October 15, 1969, seven months after the general elections, the president, Abdirashiid Ali Shermaarke was assassinated while he was on tour of northeast Somalia. Six days later, a group of military officers led by Maj. Gen. Muhammad Siad Barre took advantage of the chaos that resulted from the assassination and took power. Siad Barre dissolved the elected government and appointed himself president of the republic. The Supreme Revolutionary Council, made up of members of the military, replaced the National Assembly. The National Security Service was created to function as a police force with the power to arrest and discipline anyone who opposed the regime.

Under General Barre many Somalis were arrested, convicted, and imprisoned without due process of law.

At first the Somali people welcomed and supported the new administration, hoping that the military government would eradicate corruption and work in the interest of all Somalis. The goal of the regime as announced by Siad Barre was simply to do the people's will. He said his government would transform and better the lives of his people through the elimination of the clan conflicts (tribalism) that had always defined Somali political life.

The fight against tribalism became a hallmark of Siad Barre's rule. In a speech given in 1974, Siad Barre argued that the enemy to the stability and progress of Somalia was tribalism.

> The most explosive arsenal is TRIBALISM which benefits the reactionaries that care the least about the progress of their nation. I urge all Somalis to wage a war against tribalism and [to] spearhead the struggle against this social evil that is contrary to our unity and socialist belief, in order to enhance our future chances of social, economic and technical achievements.[12]

The people hailed Siad Barre as their savior. But unfortunately the regime succumbed to the clan loyalties and squabbles that had always characterized Somali politics and society.

THE FALL OF SIAD BARRE'S REGIME

By 1975, the Somali people were becoming increasingly disenchanted with Siad Barre's administration. It appeared that Siad Barre had no plans to restore the country to a democratically elected government. Despite his promises to eliminate tribalism in government, the general public noted that the people surrounding the president were members of his lineage. His son-in-law was head of the powerful and much feared National Security Service; his maternal uncle had the position of the head of the Supreme Revolutionary Council. I. M. Lewis reports that "in 1974 (and up to 1986), the clandestine code name for the military regime was MOD. M stands for the president's patrilineage (Marrehan); O for that of his mother (Ogaden); and D for the Dulbahante, the lineage of his son-in-law."[13]

In addition to its failure to live up to its promises, Siad Barre's government made other serious mistakes. The president had abolished Islamic law on the basis that such laws fostered division among the people. Unsurprisingly, the

A large poster of Siad Barre covers the wall of a building in Somalia. Many people became disenchanted with Barre's rule when it became clear that he was not going to restore Somalia to democracy.

displaced elders and religious leaders were displeased with this move. Further alienating the nation's religious leaders, the president gave a decree granting women equal rights to inheritance and equal representation under the law. In a nation where women are considered second-class citizens, such a change was bound to be controversial.

In response to what the people saw as the erosion of their culture by the president, a number of political groups sprang up in opposition to the government. Siad Barre's response was to tighten his hold on the government and initiate a campaign to intimidate the opposition. Political opponents were arrested and imprisoned without trial; some were accused of sabotage and were summarily executed. To distract opposition and build patriotic support for his regime, Siad Barre entered into a war with Ethiopia over the Ogaden region.

THE OGADEN WAR

In 1977, the Somali military, with modern equipment supplied by the Soviet Union, launched a war against Ethiopian forces in the Ogaden region. At the outset, Somali forces scored a series of victories against the Ethiopians. In the eu-

A Somali guerilla stands in front of an Ethiopian fort captured during the war in the Ogaden.

phoria that followed these initial successes, the Somali people once more united in support of Siad Barre. The Somali military success against Ethiopia, however, was short-lived. In 1978, Ethiopian forces, aided by Soviet and Cuban fighters, launched a series of counterattacks that finally weakened the Somali soldiers and forced them out of the Ogaden territory. By April 1978, the war was over. Somalia had failed to regain the Ogaden.

THE SOMALI CIVIL WAR

Immediately after the Ogaden War, in April 1978, a group of military officers from northern Somalia launched an unsuccessful coup against Siad Barre's government. Those arrested were executed; those who escaped fled to Ethiopia. There, they formed the first organized opposition to the Somali government, Somali Democratic Salvation Front (SSDF). Soon other groups, the Somali National Movement (SNM) and the United Somali Congress (USC) emerged to join the opposition.

Despite repression by the military regime, the activities of the opposition groups intensified. The fighting between opposition groups and armed government supporters reached massive proportions in 1988, when a bloody confrontation between members of the SNM and government forces laid waste the northern part of Somalia. SNM had hoped to capture Hargeysa, the largest city in the north, and to use it as a base for its guerilla attacks on the government. Siad Barre responded with air raids that left 70 percent of Hargeysa in ruins.

SNM forces fled to the countryside and from there continued guerilla attacks on the government. Lawlessness and chaos ruled in the north following the Hargeysa battle. Armed men roamed the country, terrorizing the civilian population.

By 1989 the fighting had spread to the south with violent clashes between government troops and the southern-based United Somali Congress. By mid-1990, chaos and terror reigned in the region. Many demonstrations and riots resulted in bloody confrontations between demonstrators and government troops. Repression by the regime continued with the arrest and execution without trial of

FEAR

Jama Osman Samater was in Hargeysa during the government's air attack of 1988. He describes his experience:

We stayed in Hargeysa until June 8. My wife, mother, six children, two sisters and their children gathered in one house. After a few days, the shelling started. It was relentless. They shelled homes, even when no one was in the house. The objective was to ensure that no one escaped alive and no house left to stand. Volleys of artillery were being fired from every direction. There was burning everywhere. In front of my sister's house, a wooden house was hit and eight people, mostly women and children, perished. The shock was so overwhelming that we soon lost any sense of fear. . . . [E]veryone was a victim. The shelling did not discriminate. There were even dead animals, dogs, and goats, everywhere. The first dead bodies I saw were two or three traders of Asian origin who had lived in Somalia for generations. I went to hide in a mosque. I couldn't walk fast as there were so many dead bodies on the road.

many opponents. The capital of Mogadishu was a war zone, with members of the USC closing in on government headquarters.

Early in 1991, Siad Barre and remnants of his supporters fled Mogadishu for the protection of his kinsmen in the Gedo region. Sixteen months later (May 1992), Siad Barre fled to Nigeria. Thousands of Somalis lost their lives during the civil war, and more than a million had fled as refugees into neighboring countries.

Despite the departure of Siad Barre, peace was elusive. A power struggle ensued between the various factions within the opposition. Making matters worse, famine overran most of the region in 1992 and 1993, claiming three hundred thousand lives. What little government remained was impotent in the face of continued warfare between the clans that were backing the various opponents of the failed regime. It seemed that nobody could halt Somalia's slide into anarchy. Warlords, backed by the armed members of their respective clans, were in charge of Somalia.

THE ROLE OF THE UNITED NATIONS: OPERATION RESTORE HOPE

In 1992 the United Nations was forced to look at the Somali situation, after a massive media campaign initiated by international human rights organizations bombarded television viewers with pictures of ruined cities, starving children, and armed Somali thugs and militia wandering the streets of Mogadishu.

On January 23, 1992, the United Nations adopted its first resolution on Somalia, calling for a complete arms embargo and a cease-fire. It also called for massive aid to prevent starvation among famine-stricken Somalis. A United Nations envoy was sent to help in the delivery of the humanitarian aid and to initiate talks between the warring factions within the country. In response, the parties agreed to a cease-fire and negotiations.

However, a cease-fire does not always mean that animosities end. It was obvious to the United Nations personnel in Somalia that a United Nations military force was needed to maintain the peace and keep order. The first United Nations troops arrived in Somalia in September 1992. This was followed by twenty-five thousand U.S. Marines sent by President

George Bush in November to help the United Nations distribute food and maintain stability in the nation. The Somali peacekeeping mission was called Operation Restore Hope.

Although intentions were good, the United Nations force, for the most part, was ill-prepared for the work it was asked to do. In just over a year, the United States began to withdraw its troops from Somalia. By March 1994, barely fifteen months into the peacekeeping mission, the U.S. soldiers

During Operation Restore Hope, United States Marines were sent to Somalia to help the United Nations distribute food and keep the peace.

THE TRAGEDY

The United Nations envoy to Somalia in 1992, Muhammad Sahnoun, describes his impression of Mogadishu when he arrived to lead the United Nations in establishing peace in the region. He states:

> When I arrived in Mogadishu in March 1992, on a fact-finding mission, the city was nearly deserted. Most people had fled to the surrounding areas, where they lived in the worst of conditions and many faced death by starvation. Despite the cease-fire agreement, fighting still occurred periodically around Mogadishu. These skirmishes seemed grotesque in view of the tragedy and chaos in the country as a whole. At least 300,000 people had died of hunger and hunger-related diseases, and thousands more were casualties of the repression and the civil war. Seventy percent of the country's livestock had been lost, and the farming areas had been devastated, compelling the farming population to seek refuge in remote areas or across the border in refugee camps. Some 500,000 people were in camps in Ethiopia, Kenya, and Djibouti. More than 3,000—mostly women, children, and old men—were dying daily from starvation. That was the tragic situation in Somalia at the beginning of 1992.

were completely out of the region. A few United Nations personnel stayed behind to help with food distribution, but, for the most part, the Somalis were left alone to decide the fate of their country.

The civil war and the breakdown of the Somali state has had profound effects on many levels. It deepened wounds already existing within different segments of the population and introduced new animosities. After many peace conferences and treaties initiated both by the Somali warlords and the international community, the Somalis have yet to rebuild their nation. The country is currently divided into three major political regions—north, northeast, and south. In the south, different factions of the Somali militia engage in daily armed conflicts over regional boundaries. Many Somali citizens are still living in exile in neighboring African countries and other parts of the world.

5

Just Getting By:
Living and Working
in Somalia

Seven decades of imperial rule by Italy and Britain significantly changed the face of Somali politics and the country's relationship to the outside world. But colonial rule left Somali economic institutions virtually untouched. Somalia is one of the poorest countries in Africa. Its economy functions at a minimal subsistence level. Most Somalis live much as their ancestors have lived for centuries, as pastoral nomads and farmers. Wealth is still, for the most part, based on the number of livestock, camels, cattle, sheep, and goats a person owns. In rural areas, lack of sufficient food production means that people starve or rely heavily on international relief agencies for food. In the cities, imported food is available. But as recent travelers to Somalia indicate, only the very rich, which excludes most Somalis, can afford to buy imported products. The Somalis are struggling just to get by.

Modes of Livelihood

Methods of earning a living in Somalia follow three traditional patterns: pastoral nomadism, farming, and nonagricultural work. Nomads and farmers make up 82 percent of the work force; merchants, civil servants, and those employed by the manufacturing industries constitute the remainder.

The type of work one does in Somalia determines in which region of the country one lives. The nomads live mainly in the north, where the land is suitable for herding animals, although they occasionally wander through the south in search of water and pasture during the dry season. The farmers live in the northwest in the Woqooyi Galbeed region, where rainfall is regular, and in the southern regions where two rivers, the Shabeelle and the Jubba, and higher rainfall make cultivation feasible. The civil servants, merchants, and others involved in the nonagricultural sector mostly settle in the coastal cities.

PASTORAL NOMADS

Roughly 60 to 70 percent of Somalis are pastoral nomads. Being a nomad for the Somali is not just an occupation, it is a way of life. Their lifestyle consists of herding animals across the land in search of water and pasture. The nomads raise sheep, goats, and camels, but the camel is the nomad's most prized possession. His wealth and status in society are determined by the number of camels he owns. The camel's high

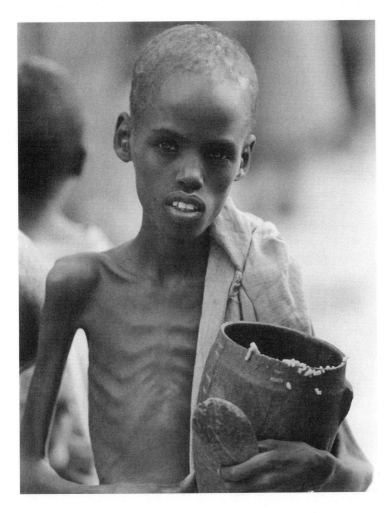

Hunger is a large part of Somali life. Here a young boy walks away from a Red Cross food distribution point.

regard in Somali society comes from the fact that it serves so many purposes. It is the primary mode of transportation for goods. A camel produces a great deal of milk, at times making it the only reliable source of nutrition for the Somali nomad and his family. And, most importantly, the camel is capable of surviving and flourishing in the harsh arid climate of Somalia. Camels require little or no tending to survive and can go for weeks (20–25 days) without water. Because of its value, the camel still serves as the basic form of payment for dowry as well as for blood compensation in Somali society.

Nomads, by definition, move frequently, which leads Somalis to regard land ownership somewhat flexibly. As B. W. Andrzejewski and I. M. Lewis state, "Pasture is regarded as a gift of God to all Somalis: and is not viewed as parceled out amongst specific groups."[14] As such, even though individual clans lay claim to various segments of land, boundaries are not clearly defined. Any open space is considered free for possession and occupation at any time.

 ## CAMELS: VERSATILE AND VALUABLE

According to scholar Said Samatar, there are many reasons why the camel is an important part of Somali culture:

> The Somali nomads' interest in the camel and their love of it is entirely pragmatic. If they cherish it, it is because this generous beast does not fail them. To begin with, the camel is the only domestic animal that does not require a large quantity of the one resource which is so scarce in Somalia: water. In the hottest, driest period, the camel needs to be watered once every 20–25 days. In the rainy season, given the fresh supply of green pasturage, the camel need not be watered at all.

> Come rain or drought, the camel's generosity to man is crucial to his survival. The she-camel's milk is delicious, refreshing and thirst-quenching; her meat is tasty and tender like veal; her skin is utilized as draperies for the nomadic hut which shelters the Somalis from the elements. The burden-bearing he-camel is the main transport vehicle and carries the children, the aged, the sick and the nomad's belongings for hundreds of miles every year.

The fluidity of land ownership has always been a point of conflict between different clans and families. Anthropologists Carol Beckwith and Angela Fisher, who traveled through the Horn of Africa studying and recording the daily lives of the people, state that

A nomad constructs a dwelling within his camp. Several nomadic families will generally travel together in order to defend livestock and land.

> in traditional Somali society, it was a simple fact of life that if new pastures could be occupied by force of arms, then they would be occupied; conversely if territory that one clan had made its own by customary usage could not be defended, then others would certainly encroach upon it. Running through the entire culture, even today, is a firm belief that might is right: in all circumstances, the strong win and the weak lose.[15]

Such a belief system makes small groups vulnerable to attacks. Consequently, the Somali nomads do not travel alone. It is unusual to see a nomadic family traveling by itself. The norm is for several nomadic families to combine and travel together. The group of families camps together, and in addition to grazing their animals collectively, they defend their camp against raiders.

The nomadic camp is called a hamlet, *aqal* in the Somali language. An average camp contains three to six nuclear families. The married men of the camp are often members of the same lineage or *diya*-paying group. Each married woman or widow lives in her own dwelling along with her children. The dwellings themselves are beehive-like tents made from mats and animal skins over a framework of branches. The tents are collapsible and can easily be dismantled and packed on the back of a camel whenever it is time to move on.

Tents are arranged in a circular manner within the camp. At the center are thorn bush pens where livestock, especially sheep and goats, are kept during the night. The encampment itself is surrounded by a fence of wild thorn branches to keep predators and other unwanted visitors away at night.

The nomads have very few material possessions. Inside the tents are usually two portable beds lying on either side of the entrance. On the floor, one may find various wood and fiber containers for water and milk, plates, pots, pans, and food—sugar, tea, dates, rice, and sorghum. Small utensils such as wooden milk jugs and finely carved wooden beakers for serving coffee, milk, or water are stored in the framework of the house.

A HARD LIFE

Somali nomads follow a strict division of labor based on gender. The women are generally responsible for loading and unloading the camels and for erecting the tents. They stay close to the hamlets and attend to household needs as well as looking after the domestic livestock, mainly goats and sheep. Men usually assist women at the wells or water holes when the sheep and goats are watered. But the primary responsibility of the men, and their real focus of attention, is the grazing camels, which are usually located away from the hamlets.

Very few nomadic children go to school, and those who do are usually sent to live with relatives in the cities. Most stay with their parents and help them care for the animals. Girls stay at home helping their mothers with domestic chores until they marry. Boys from the age of seven are sent out with the young men to the camel-grazing sites, called camel-camps,

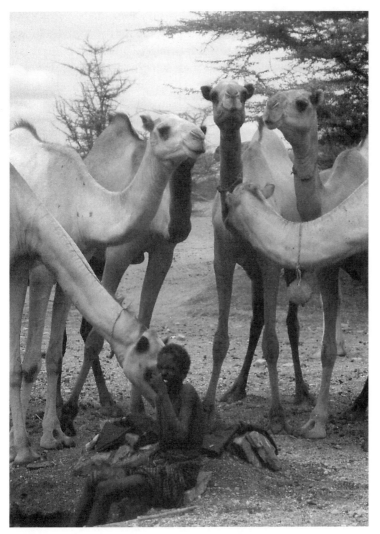

Somali camel-boys learn from a young age the skills needed for a nomadic life.

where they help care for the animals and learn from their elders about the hard work of being a nomad.

The camel-boys, as they are called, rarely have a roof of any kind over their heads. They sleep out under the stars on thin mats, protected from the cold of the desert nights only by the clothes they wear. They are often without the means to cook, their main diet consisting of camel milk, drunk three times daily. From such experiences, say Carol Beckwith and Angela Fisher, the camel-boys quickly acquire all the skills and values that will stand them in good stead in later life. They learn which are the best pastures and which grasses can endanger their stock. They learn basic veterinary procedures, how to manage the herds, and to love and care for the individual animals in their charge. Most important of all, in a land that has only two perennial rivers, they learn where to find water. Ibrahim Ismaa'il, a Somali from the Darood clan, describes his life as a camel-boy. He says,

> following the camels from one pasture to another, we always used to sleep away from the *rerr,* in the open; when nights were cold we slept among the camels. Rain did not disturb my slumber: very exceptionally would we seek the shelter of a neighboring hut. We got up at the break of dawn and walked until the heat of the sun became too strong, when both animals and men would seek refuge and rest under the shade of trees. Our food consisted almost entirely of camel's milk, which we used to drink three times a day. Meat was occasionally indulged in when a camel had met with an accident and had to be killed, or when an antelope or some other game had been caught. Gum arabic we used to suck as a sweetmeat. Then we used to pick and eat a variety of wild fruit.[16]

With such a frugal and arduous existence, it is perhaps not surprising that life expectancy for the Somali nomad, estimated at 47 years, ranks among the lowest in the world. Even during the best of times, when water is abundant and there is enough pasture for the animals, nomads still function at a minimum subsistence level. During the dry season, when milk is scarce, the nomad's life is particularly hard. In addition to the long treks that they have to undertake at regular intervals in the dry seasons to water camels, and the frequent moves from pasture to pasture, nomads have to be constantly on the alert for raids by hostile clans or attacks by wild animals. Should a prolonged drought or other natural or human-made disaster occur, the result for the nomad is famine. In 1974–1975 when a drought gripped northern Africa, about ten thousand Somalis died. The 1984–1985 drought claimed about seven thousand Somalis. The 1992–1993 drought, in conjunction with the violent conflicts that were then ravaging the country, is estimated to have claimed about three hundred thousand Somali lives.

Because of the harsh reality of life for the nomads, the international community has made repeated attempts to resettle them. But for the proud Somalis, resettlement has not been easy or tempting. It is difficult to abandon one's ancestors' way of life, especially if one's identity is interwoven with it.

FARMING

Farming forms the second mode of livelihood in Somalia. Most Somali farmers are semipastoralists, which means that they combine cultivation of crops with raising livestock, especially sheep, goats, cattle, and a few camels.

However, unlike the nomads, the farmers live in permanent villages and communities. Farming communities vary in size from several to a few hundred nuclear families. Each family lives in a round mud house built on their farm. Children in farming communities, like their nomadic counterparts, spend much of their time helping their parents. The children tend to the domestic animals, watering them at the rivers or at ponds built for the purpose. They also help plant, weed, and carry home the

Farming remains the second most common occupation in Somalia. Here Somali women harvest a grain crop.

crops after harvest, and prepare them for market. During the dry season, they often have to undertake long treks to find water for their livestock and the family.

In the northwest, near the town of Hargeysa in the region called Woqooyi Galbeed, farmers engage in what is called dryland cultivation. With average annual rainfall of twenty inches and no other water sources except deep wells, farmers grow crops like corn and millet, which do not need much water to survive.

The larger population of farmers is concentrated in the south. Near the Jubba and Shabeelle Rivers, irrigation is possible and farmers can grow a variety of crops. The region provides two forms of traditional cultivation: dry farming of corn and millet on the upland soils of the interior and wet farming of sugarcane, cotton, bananas, and rice on the rich irrigated soils of the river basins.

Until the civil war destroyed the economy, sugarcane plantations along the river basins produced enough sugar for Somalia's domestic consumption as well as for export. Bananas produced by the southern farmers consituted the country's number one cash crop. Cotton was also produced in high quantities, although its annual yield was still low compared to that of other countries. Recently, as some Somalis who fled their homeland during the civil war return home, the farming villages are making efforts to rebuild their communities and restart their lives. Agricultural production, however, is still not up to prewar levels.

Somalia has always had very few factories, most of which were involved in the processing of agricultural products. There was a textile factory, a skin and hide processing industry, and a number of dairies and sugar refineries. These factories, however, were destroyed during the civil war.

TRADING

Every Somali engages in one form of trading or another. Nomads must sell their animal products to buy things they do not produce, such as sugar and tea. Farmers must sell some of their produce to buy clothes and other manufactured goods. But nomads and farmers do not consider themselves traders. The name is reserved for

those who spend the greater part of their daily lives as merchants.

Merchants live mostly in the coastal cities, which have for centuries been famed as centers of trade. Merchants engage in local trading with the people of Somalia as well as in trade with other countries of the world, including India, Egypt, Ethiopia, Italy, and countries of the Arabian Peninsula. They export Somali products like skins, hides, ivory, myrrh, and frankincense. They import manufactured goods, electronic equipment, oil, and food products not produced in sufficient quantities in the country itself.

Somali merchants carry on trade both within their country and outside it in neighboring countries.

The Middlemen

A group of merchants known as small-scale traders serve the role of the middleman between those living in the rural areas and the urban population. They travel back and forth between the rural areas and the cities buying and selling products, and they often have no permanent stores. While in the city, merchants buy materials and foodstuffs, such as tea, oil, and rice, that are needed in the rural areas. They load these items in a truck and transport them to rural markets where they are resold. Before returning to the city, they buy local goods such as livestock, skins, hides, hand-made goods, and spices. These are sold in the city for local consumption or to other merchants for eventual export.

In the city, people trade using the Somali currency, the Somali shilling, or if they can get them, American dollars.

A craftsman in rural Somalia fashions a large basket. Small-scale traders will purchase goods such as this and transport them to the city for resale.

CAMPAIGN FOR LITERACY

During the 1970s, the failed regime of Muhammad Siad Barre undertook a massive campaign for literacy
among the Somalis. He argued that illiteracy, which was syn-
onymous with "ignorance" in his opinion, was the root of tribalism, clan animosities, and the weak Somali economy. At that
time, barely 5 percent of the Somali population could read
and write, and Somali was still only a spoken language. Thus,
a nationwide literary campaign (the Rural Development Campaign) to educate the Somali people was launched in July
1974. The program sent literate high school students and their
teachers (about thirty thousand) to the rural areas to teach the
people how to read and write. When the crash program ended
six months later, the government claimed that roughly
1,759,000 Somalis who could not read or write before the campaign were then able to do so. The number constituted 30 percent of the Somali population. Thirty percent might seem
relatively small when compared to western nations, but for Somalia it was a good beginning and a significant development.

In rural areas, however, where money is often scarce, nomads use local products such as livestock, skins, and
hides as forms of currency. These are particularly desir-
able currency from the point of view of merchants because they can be resold in the cities at significant profits.

Unlike the small-scale traders, most city merchants have
permanent shops in private buildings or open markets from
which they sell their products. From the time shops open,
usually at around 8 A.M., there is no end to the shoppers and
businessmen and women who fill the streets and the open-
air markets looking for bargains. Prices in Somali stores are
not preset, and a buyer knows that he or she must haggle
with the seller to reach a good price. This makes the Somali
shops and markets rather lively places as people haggle over
prices and transact business.

By noon the heat makes serious activities almost impossible, and most Somalis retire to their homes for an afternoon
nap. Some store owners close their stores at noon and reopen
around 3 P.M. From 3 P.M. to sunset is as busy as the morning
hours, with people buying, selling, and carrying out other
business transactions.

CRAFT-WORK

Even though the preference among Somalis who live in towns is to earn a living through trading, there is a smaller group who earn their living as craftspeople and artisans. Many Somalis, including farmers and nomads, engage in crafts in an informal way. Women make mats when they are not helping with the animals or working on the farms; and men make fiber and wooden household utensils during their leisure time. But rarely are these products sold for money. Craft-making as a profession seems to be reserved for a couple of Somali clans, the Tumal and the Yibir. The Tumal are mostly blacksmiths. They produce tools like knives, swords, spears, and hatchets. The Yibir mostly work with leather, making prayer mats, amulets, shoes, wallets, and straps from animal hides.

SCHOOL IN SOMALIA

Somalis' reliance on traditional modes of earning a living creates an economy that adversely affects its communication and educational systems. Access to rural areas is still mostly by foot or by unreliable trucks that travel on dangerous dirt roads. Often during the rainy seasons, most roads are impassible even for trucks.

Children who live in rural areas rarely have opportunities to go to school; and while those who live in the cities are more likely to go to school, few attend beyond the elementary grades. Before the civil war that basically destroyed the school system, about 50 percent of Somali children were enrolled in elementary schools; but a mere 7 percent were enrolled in high school.

There were also vocational schools for students who wanted to obtain technical skills, such as in agriculture, mechanics, masonry, or forestry. Those wanting to further their education beyond the secondary and vocational school level had a choice of teacher training colleges, a school of nursing, the School of Polytechnics, or the Somali National University in Mogadishu. Few, however, took advantage of the educational opportunities. A mere four thousand students were enrolled in the Somali National University before the complete collapse of the Somali government in 1992.

The Somalis' general lack of access to education contributes to the nation's weak economy. It means that the country, at least for the foreseeable future, will continue to lack a skilled, educated workforce equipped to rebuild the economy.

Those who bear the brunt of the burden of the harsh life are the children. Infant mortality is high: more than 12 percent of Somali children die before the age of five. Those who survive past the age of five face the arduous life that traditional patterns of livelihood force upon Somalis; reliant as they are on an inhospitable environment, older children face a constant fear of starvation.

6

A RICH ARTISTIC HERITAGE

Despite its weak economy and current political problems, Somalia is still culturally strong. This strength is seen not only in the resilience of its traditional institutions but also in its arts. No account of Somali society and culture would be complete without some mention of the role and character of the Somali artistic heritage.

Somali values and culture underlie their artistic heritage; their stories, proverbs, poetry, pottery, leather, and woodwork express their understanding of the intricate workings of their world, their struggles to survive, their religion, their relationship to and view of the outside world, and their unshaken belief in the value of their traditions. In this way, the Somali people's cultural identity and their arts are inextricably intertwined. Some scholars say that the rich Somali artistic tradition is perhaps the most pronounced achievement of Somalia.

FOLKLORE

The fact that Somali functioned primarily as an oral language for centuries contributed to the Somali people's fascination with and appreciation of the spoken word. Storytelling, therefore, is an important part of Somali life. Somali fables, legends, and myths are designed to instruct as well as entertain. The lessons they teach range from how to survive in society to an explanation of natural events. While the stories are regional in content and tone, the lessons they teach are universal.

The favorite time to tell stories is in the evening when the day's chores are done. The old and the young come together to reminisce over the day's activities and entertain one another with tales. "Lessons learned in this way are hard to forget," the Somalis say.

PROVERBS

Like storytelling, proverbs play a special role in Somali daily life. One Somali man notes that proverbs "put spice into speech."[17] Every gathering in Somalia is an occasion for the use of proverbs. People often converse solely in proverbs for the intellectual amusement and appreciation of the listeners.

The beauty and power of proverbs is that they allow people to express themselves using images from life to draw attention to the topic being discussed without being blunt. For among the Somalis, "It is considered to be a sign of refinement and wisdom not to come directly to the point," states B. W. Andrzejewski, a leading scholar of the Somali language,

but to present to the audience one's statements or proposals by means of allegorical images, veiled expressions and cryptic allusions, which are subsumed under the term *guudmar* which literally means "moving over (or above) the surface" and is contrasted with the term *gudagal* "entering inside," i.e., dealing with the subject matter directly.[18]

Somali women sit weaving baskets within a house. The rich Somali artistic tradition is perhaps the greatest achievement of Somalia.

Because of the role of proverbs in Somali social interaction, every Somali is not only expected to be skilled in using proverbs, but in understanding their meanings as well. For as another proverb says, "When you tell a fool a proverb, he will ask you for its meaning."

Some proverbs simply express life the way the Somalis see it. Proverbs such as "Someone who is ill can order a hundred people about" and "Wherever you win someone for yourself, you also lose someone" express general notions about human relationships. The majority of the proverbs, however, serve the primary function of instruction. For example, a child who is caught lying could be told, "Lies are honey at first; later they are myrrh [a bitter, bad-tasting herb]." A person who often gets himself in danger could be told, "Fools carry in the crook of their arm the rope with which someone will tie them up."

Somali proverbs use images that come from the Somali environment and way of life. Andrzejewski notes that be-

ABUNAWAS THE TRICKSTER

A favorite collection of Somali tales tells the story of the trickster Abunawas who always finds a way to outsmart his opponents. One of the stories, called "Abunawas and the Merchant," goes like this:

Abunawas built a two-story house and wanted to sell it. For a long time, no one wanted to buy the house. Then one day a merchant came along and agreed to buy the top story. Matters remained like this for a long time until one day Abunawas, again, wanted to sell the whole house. He asked the merchant to buy the first story, but the merchant refused, saying he was completely happy living on the second story. Abunawas thought about the situation for a long time. Finding no one else interested in buying the house, he devised a plan. One day, he hired some workers and brought them to his house. He then called out to the merchant who lived on the second story of the house and said to him, "I want to break up my house below, so you look after your house above, and don't come and say I didn't tell you." The merchant did not know what to do. He then relented and bought the house from Abunawas at a great price. That's how Abunawas outsmarted the merchant and sold his house.

cause domestic and wild animals and desert plants feature prominently in Somali life, they appear often in the proverbs. Other proverbs, such as "The camel which is behind keeps the pace of the one in front"; "Sheep and goats stampede for a false reason, but they do not limp for a false reason"; and "Of the lion which keeps quiet and the lion which roars, the one which roars is better," can only come from a people who understand animal life and have an intimate relationship with the natural world. Thus, in a very important way, proverbs not only promote and celebrate the Somalis' appreciation of and preoccupation with linguistic skills, they reinforce the people's way of life.

Somalis' proverbs use images drawn from their environment and way of life.

POETRY

While folklore and proverbs feature prominently in Somali life, spoken poetry plays an even larger role in the country's culture. Somalia, as every person acquainted with the country emphasizes, is a nation of poets. Unlike most societies, where poetry is the province of relatively few individuals, interest in poetry in Somalia is universal. Poetry, says I. M. Lewis, is a living force intimately connected with all aspects of everyday life in Somalia. One famous Somali poet, Sayid Maxamed Cabdulle Xasan, called poetry a precious jewel.

Somali poems rely heavily on alliteration and as such are easy to memorize and to remember. Poems travel great distances with people who have memorized them and recite them frequently. During their travels in Somalia, B. W. Andrjewski and I. M. Lewis were struck by the powerful memory of the Somalis in relationship to their poetry. "Unaided by writing, they learn long poems by heart and some have repertoires which are too great to be exhausted even by several evenings of continuous recitation. Some of them are endowed with such powers of memory that they can learn a poem by heart hearing it only once, which is quite astonishing."[19]

Poems are chanted slowly and important lines sometimes repeated to aid memorization. The reciters, says Lewis, are not only capable of acquiring a wide repertoire but can store it in their memories for many years, sometimes for a lifetime. There are poets who at a ripe age could still remember many poems which they learned as children. Ali Abdi, a Somali from the Darood clan, remembers that his grandfather had a substantial amount of poems committed to memory. "We used to sit down many evenings and just listen to him recite poems after poems. He knew the importance of these poems and he wanted to pass them on to us."[20]

AN UNWRITTEN COPYRIGHT LAW

Having good memory and knowing the importance of their poetry is one reason for the preservation of a substantial amount of Somali poetry. Another reason is the unwritten Somali copyright law. Unlike other countries, where oral literature is anonymous and the property of society, the Somalis developed a system by which poets had an unwritten copyright protection for their work. Anyone who memorized someone else's poem and wanted to recite it afterwards was obligated to remember the text accurately and to reproduce it faithfully at each recital. The reciter had to give the name of the original composer at each recital. Failure to give the name of the author or giving wrong credit was considered a serious breach of ethical code and punishable according to customary laws. The Somalis consider appropriating some-

A LIVING ART

In his book *Oral Poetry and Somali Nationalism,* the Somali-born scholar Said Samatar discusses the preeminent position Somali poetry occupies in Somali life. He writes:

> What, then, makes the poetry such a pervasive force in Somali Society? To the Somalis the question is not so difficult to answer: poetry is the medium whereby an individual or a group can present a case most persuasively. The pastoralist poet, to borrow a phrase, is the public relations man of the clan, and through his craft he exercises a powerful influence in clan affairs. Unlike Western poetry, which appears to be primarily a concern of a group of professionals dealing with, more often than not, a subject matter intended for the members of what seems a small, highly literate section of society, Somali pastoral verse is a living art affecting almost every aspect of life. Its functions are versatile, concerned not only with matters of art and aesthetics but also with questions of social significance. It illuminates culture, society, and history.

one's work as the equivalent of theft. A person breaking copyright laws paid a fine to the wronged party in money or livestock, and was considered a disgrace to the community. Thus, Somali copyright protection, though unwritten, ensured the survival of great poetry and the acknowledgment of the authors.

Beyond its aesthetic and entertainment value, poetry serves many social and political purposes for the Somalis. Poetry provides Somalis a way to probe the essence of existence. Said Samatar, a Somali, says that poetry equips the Somalis with the methods and means to articulate the abiding questions: Where do we come from? What are we? Where are we going? When they talk of poetry, Somalis have in mind something which embodies the totality of their cultural existence and to which they attach the highest measure of importance. In the words of one elder, "Poetry is the central integrating principle without which harmonious relationships in society would be unthinkable."[21]

Poetry also functions to preserve the Somali cultural heritage. For a long time, the Somali language was primarily oral; there were no books, journals, or newspapers to record and preserve the people's history. Poetry became the means to do so, serving as the principal medium of mass communication in the country. The importance of poetry to Somali culture is so strong that even today, when a written form of the Somali language has been developed and newspapers, radio, and television are available, this role continues to serve its traditional mass communication role. This is partly because most Somalis cannot read and write and still rely on the spoken word. The other reason is the Somalis' undying appreciation of the spoken word.

Every clan or lineage has its own leading poet who serves as the voice of the people. The poet composes poetry to record events, to influence the opinion of the people on a particular matter, to express the people's opinion, or to simply comment upon the issue at hand as the poet sees it.

Because of the cultural value of poetry and the fact that there are many poets among the Somalis, competition for the public ear is often fierce. Poets often criticize each other's work while extolling the greatness of their own verse. Poetry contests are held every year in spring. Each clan presents its best poets and their group of memorizers, called *Hafidayaal*, whose task is to disseminate and preserve for posterity the works of the master poets who do verbal battle with opponents from rival clans. The contest is judged by a panel of elders recognized for their mastery of the art of literary criticism and for giving impartial decisions. Prizes are given to the best half-dozen or so poets. Prizes range from a token gift, such as a spear or a piece of cloth, to half a dozen camels. But the greatest honor the poet receives is being considered one of the best poets of the land.

POETRY'S POLITICAL POWER

Somali poets wield great political power. Skill in composing poetry is considered as valuable as skill in wielding weapons. This is because poetry has the power to incite wars, like a direct attack on the enemy. As Said Samatar indicates, an insult or slander in poetry is considered to have the same effect on the victim as a physical assault, and poetic slander has been the source of many lethal interclan feuds. Usually wars between clans are carried out on a very charged intellectual level between their poets even before any arms are raised. And during wars, poetry is also used to pour insults and abuse on the opponents and to raise the morale of the poet's warriors. Ali Duuh, in a poem entitled "Lament," enumerates all the evils heaped upon his people by a rival clan and angrily chides his people about their indifference, inciting them to action. "Fate is like the clouds of the sky, and like the wind," he says.

> There is no one to do anything about misfortune,
> about the debt (of compensation for those who
> were killed).
> Vicissitudes of fortune drive on the warriors . . .
> If you are not weaklings, your chance for revenge
> has come.
> I want you to fight, in an issue which should
> concern you.
> Arise, you fools, from the place where you idly sit, your
> lips drooping![22]

Poetry can also be used as an instrument for reconciling clan rivalries. One folktale celebrates the role of Salaan Arrabey's poem "Oh Clansmen, Stop the War" in ending a violent feud between two rival sections of the Isaaq clan. According to the story, the poet on his horse stood between the massed opposing forces, and with a voice charged with drama and emotion, chanted the better part of the day until the men, overcome by the force of his oratory, dropped their weapons and embraced each other.

TYPES OF SOMALI POETRY

Somalis classify their poems into distinct types, depending on a poem's purpose. *Gabay, jiifto,* and *geeraar* are Somali's classical poetry and are used to express serious political, philosophical, and religious themes. The *gabay, jiifto,* and *geeraar* are poems of public forum used to teach, incite people to action or mediate peace between rival parties. One man who demonstrates the power of the Somali classical poetry is the late Sayyid Muhammad ibn 'Abd Allah Hasan, termed the "Mad Mullah of Somalia" by the British during colonial rule. Hasan despised the colonization of his country by Europeans and used his poetry to galvanize the people against colonial rule. In one poem, he tells the British:

> I have no forts, no houses
> I have no cultivated fields, no silver or gold
> for you to take. . . . The country is bush . . .
> If you want wood and stone, you get them in plenty.
> There are also many termite hills.
> The sun is very hot.
> All you can get from me is war . . .
> If you want peace, go away from my country . . .[23]

Sometimes classical poetry is also used to make personal commentary on a public matter, as seen in the poem "Our Country is Divided" by Farrar Nuur:

 ## THE POWER OF POETRY

The poem "Oh Clansmen, Stop the War" was used by the Somali poet Salaan Arrabey to reconcile two rival groups with the Isaaq clan gearing for battle over some old feud. In the poem, the poet reminds the clan about the evils of war. The poem was powerful enough to make the groups reconsider their positions and seek reconciliation. Here is an excerpt from the lengthy poem, which appears in full in *Somali Poetry: An Introduction*, by B.W. Andrzejewski and I. M. Lewis:

> The day the Umar Daahir
> Cut themselves to pieces in the battle
> Of Allola'as, he who was present then
> And who also knows what happened
> At the battle of Megaag I Idan
> Knows to the full
> The horror and the turmoil of war
> And understands its real nature;
> Oh Clansmen, stop the war!
>
> He who sups plentifully every night
> Whom pride and prosperity shroud like shadeless cloud
> And damp mist mixed together,
> That in his good fortune
> He should repose in peace and tranquility
> Would be hard to credit.
> Oh Clansmen, stop the war!

The British, the Ethiopians, and the Italians
are squabbling,
The country is snatched and divided
by whosoever is stronger,
The country is sold piece by piece
without our knowledge,
And for me, all this is the teeth of
the last days of the world.[24]

Nuur wrote the poem during colonial rule, and while not as politically charged as the poetry of 'AbdAllah Hasan, it is equally powerful in expressing the disillusionment of a people under foreign rule.

The tenor of my words
He whose leaf of life has withered
And the slow-witted fool will not understand;
But when the warriors die in countless number
And the great array of men is utterly destroyed
People will soon reproach each other;
Oh Clansmen, stop the war!

Your two lineages,
Hurling boasts of strength in each other's teeth;
We are more tightly bound as kinsmen than any other group
And yet there is rancour amongst us.
We remember the battle of Anla
And the five we lost; amongst the Aadle
And the first-born son of my mother
Ans Ali Fiin, we have not forgotten,
And these killed in a desolate place
Were the kinsmen to us
And Jaama, loved by all
And our leading spokesman,
And Rabjaan, both in revelry
And in defiance of our custom you killed,
And now if you start to devour each other
I will not stand aloof
But adding my strength to one side
I shall join in the attack on the other,
Oh Clansmen, stop the war!

PERSONAL POEMS

Somalis also compose poems that celebrate events of every-day life. Such poems focus on common themes such as love, marriage, birth, death, and motherhood. The most popular of these types of poetry are the *buraambur,* or women's po-

A group of Somali women stand reciting buraambur, *a kind of poetry that deals with events of everyday life.*

etry. The recitation of poems is often accompanied with clapping, stepping, or musical instruments, such as drums and tambourines. An example is the poem "Lament for a Dead Lover," by Siraad Haad:

> You were the fierce standing between our
>
> land and the descendants of Ali,
>
> Now in your departure you give no rain
>
> while mist shrouds the world,
>
> The moon that shines no more,
>
> The risen sun extinguished,
>
> The dates on their way from Basra cut off by seas.[25]

HEELLO

The most recently developed of the Somali poetic genres is the *heello,* or mini-love poems. These poems are short, their subject matter is light, and elaborate metaphor and allegory are used to achieve meaning. Their value in Somali poetic culture is similar to that of pop music in Western societies. *Heello* is very popular among the young and is often heard over the radio, accompanied by lutes and tambourine.

DANCE AND WORK SONGS

One other category of poetry is comprised of traditional dance and work songs. These are sung at any occasion. Men sing them as they water camels; women sing them when weaving mats and performing other household chores. The poems are simple and lively. Unlike other types of Somali poems, they are anonymous. The "Camel-Watering Chant" is often sung by men as they water their camels:

> They are all here, ready,
> They belong to us
> How splendid and useful they are
> And they are standing ready
>
> . . . .
>
> I set my foot (on the wall),
> Oh Master of the world,
> Oh God the Just, make our task easy.

Somali radio broadcasts feature not only music, but also poetry. For many Somalis, poetry and music serve very similar purposes.

. . . .

You will be cooled,

. . . .

Put your mouth to it with blessing,
It is devoid of evil.
Your shriveled bones
Are now moist and full again.

. . . .

When they are standing ready,
And the clansmen are all present,
None must leave till all are watered.[26]

The rhythm and alliteration of Somali poetry are often lost in translation, but one still gets a glimpse of the beauty and power of the works. Ironically, the development of a written language and the growing use of newspapers and other forms of mass media in modern Somalia have helped to intensify rather than diminish the role of oral poetry. Somali radio, for example, carries poetry recitation the same way music is played on radio in the Western world.

VISUAL ART

While the verbal arts dominate Somali culture, observers note an intimate connection between Somali verbal and visual arts. These two elements of Somali culture nurture and sustain each other as they enhance the Somali's daily experience, according to scholar Said Samatar. Somalis are known for their skill in woodcarving, metalwork, pottery, and weaving; and these art forms are known to be long established in Somali culture. Some of the materials in private collections as well as those showcased in museums around the world have been traced back to as far as the Somali settlement of the land around the first century B.C.

Somalis strive to give every possession, no matter how functional, some aesthetic value. Even a simple camel mat is made in such a way that it blends well with the desert environment.

FOLKTALES

Somalis use folktales for instruction and entertainment. The story "The Lion's Share," from the collection of stories *The King's Drum* by Harold Courlander, teaches survival through the exercise of good judgment and learning from others' mistakes:

> The lion, the jackal, the wolf, and the hyena had a meeting and agreed that they would hunt together in one party and share equally among themselves whatever game they caught. They went out and killed a camel. The four animals then discussed which one of them would divide the meat. The lion said, "Whoever divides the meat must know how to count." Immediately the wolf volunteered, saying, "Indeed, I know how to count."
>
> He began to divide the meat. He cut off four pieces of equal size and placed one before each of the hunters. The lion was angered. He says, "Is this the way to count?" and he struck the wolf across the eyes, so that his eyes swelled up and he could not see. The jackal said, "The wolf does not know how to count. I will divide the meat." He cut three portions that were small and a fourth portion that was very large. The three small portions he placed before the hyena, the wolf, and himself. The large portion he put in front of the lion, who took his meat and went away.
>
> "Why was it necessary to give the lion such a large piece?" the hyena said. "Our agreement was to divide and share equally. Where did you ever learn how to divide?" "I learned from the wolf," the jackal answered. "Wolf? How can anyone learn from the wolf? He is stupid," the hyena said. "The jackal was right," the wolf said. "He knows how to count. Before when my eyes were open, I did not see it. Now, though my eyes are wounded, I see it clearly."

Like Somali literature and poetry, the visual arts portray unique aspects of Somali cultural history. While the arts are not lacking in aesthetic value, most of them are functional and tell the stories of the people who created them and their way of life. "Somali artists do not create just for the sake of creating or for pleasure; they create for a reason," says Somali-born scholar Said Samatar.

Each carved or woven article is never an end itself, but is rather a means to a larger cause or truth. Each object in the gallery of woodwork and woven material—the porridge bowls, spoons, milk jugs, baskets, headrests, camel bells, and watering troughs—represents a specific utilitarian function.[27]

For example, Somali women weave different types of mats for domestic as well as ornamental use. Some, brown and drab-looking, are used as camel blankets or for building the shelters used by nomads. Their sturdiness suggests that they would endure the wear and tear that comes from the nomadic way of life; and their color blends well with the natural environment of the desert land. On the other hand, there are also finely woven mats that are used for decoration and as carpets and mattresses. These are very colorful and add visual appeal to the interiors of Somali dwellings.

Somali art can also serve a symbolic function. For example, the large variety of decorative necklaces and beads which on the surface seem to have been created purely for aesthetic effect are in fact designed to make an important commentary on social relations, writes Said Samatar. The type of necklace a woman wears indicates her age and social status. As a child, she wears one kind of beads or necklace; as a teenager, another; as a young woman of marriageable age, still another. On her wedding day, she wears the marriage necklace; and as a married woman with children, she wears yet another set. The design, shape, and size of the necklaces also indicate the wealth of a woman's family. "A woman wearing a ponderous set of golden beads wants to show the world not only the wealth of her lineage, but also the costly bride-wealth a prospective candidate for her marital hand would have to provide,"[28] says Samatar.

The Somali verbal and visual arts illuminate, celebrate, and preserve the Somali cultural heritage and are undoubtedly one of the country's greatest achievements. Despite the chaos that reigns in Somalia, the country remains culturally vibrant. Outside observers puzzle over the cultural resilience of the people, noting that loyalties to their literature, poetry, and art remain as strong as ever, perhaps in some cases even stronger because of the recent ordeals.

EPILOGUE

WHAT'S NEXT FOR SOMALIA?

Somalia is at a critical stage in its history. With no central government, no public education system, no social and economic infrastructure, and no legal system, most people ask what is next for Somalia? Will the Somalis bury old and new animosities and begin the task of national building or will they allow the tragedy to continue, their country to disintegrate to the point of nonexistence? Some have suggested that the United Nations ought to play an active role in the reconstruction of Somalia, by encouraging those who fled the country during the civil war to return and providing them with the funds they need to rebuild their lives. Others, however, argue that the task of reconciliation and reconstruction must be carried out by the Somalis, that the Somalis must come together, stop killing each other, and look to the future.

Whatever happens, it is obvious that the task of rebuilding Somalia will not be easy. It will take a combined effort of the international community and the Somali people to lay the foundation for a new country. Somalis love their country, in spite of all its problems. They recognize the many things that unite them. They are one people who speak one language and share one religion. Collectively, they love the nuances of language and poetry. While Islam forms a basis through which the Somalis try to understand their world, their poetry expresses the intricate workings of their world, from clan warfare to religion to the Somalis' unshaken belief in the value of their traditions. The things that unite the Somalis and their cherished heritage make it imperative that they take the lead to reconcile their own differences and create a better nation for themselves and their children.

The most recent United Nations report on Somalia offers a hopeful outlook. It states that despite being torn to shreds by clan hostility, the basic Somali identity, religion, and culture re-

A group of Somali children stand in front of a ruined building. Despite Somalia's current situation, the people place high hopes on their unity of language and religion to help them create a better nation for themselves and their children.

main resilient. Identification with Islam remains strong, and commitment to regaining respect for Somalia in the Horn of Africa is as important now as it was a generation ago. Somalis have learned the bitter lesson that no clan can impose its will

THE BEST DANCE

In this poem, a Somali poet celebrates his culture and his people. He affirms the basic Somali belief that their society is the best in the world.

The best dance is the dance of the eastern clans,
The best people are ourselves,
Of this I have always been sure,
The best wealth is camels
The duur grass is the best fresh grazing,
The dareemo grass is the best hay,
Of this I have always been sure.

on others and that, historically, Somalis have survived precisely through decentralized power-sharing politics and systems that have emphasized checks and balances. Their cultural cohesiveness forms a substantial foundation upon which to rebuild. It is hoped that the new millennium will bring lasting peace to Somalia.

FACTS ABOUT SOMALIA

GOVERNMENT

Type: Somalia has no government at present.

1884–1960: Under colonial rule

1960–1969: Parlimentary democracy

1969–1991: Military dictatorship

1991–present: no recognized government. The United Somali Congress (USC) ousted the military regime of General Siad Barre on January 27, 1991; the present situation is one of anarchy, marked by interclan fighting.

DATES OF INDEPENDENCE

June 26, 1960, for northern Somaliland

July 1, 1960, for southern Somaliland

July 1, 1960, both northern and southern Somaliland merged to form one nation called the Democratic Republic of Somalia.

NATIONAL HOLIDAYS

May 1: Labor Day

June 26: Independence Day (northern region)

July 1: Independence Day

July 11–12: Idd El Fitr (End of Ramadan)

September 16–17: Idd El Adha

October 21–22: Revolution Day

December 16: Prophet's Birthday

PEOPLE

Population (1997, est.): 6,590,325

Major cities: Mogadishu (capital) 1,000,000; Berbera 70,000; Hargeysa 400,000; Chisimayu 200,000; Merca 100,000; Zeila 40,000

Literacy rate: 30 percent

Education: years compulsory—12 years; attendance primary—50 percent; attendance secondary—7 percent; post secondary—5 percent

Percentage of households with automobiles: 0.1 percent

Work force: 2.2 million; agriculture—82 percent; industry and commerce—13 percent; government—5 percent

Life expectancy: 47 years

Infant mortality: 145 deaths per 1,000 live births

Annual population growth: 3 percent

Population density: (1987) 18.9 per square mile

Percentage of population in cities: 20 percent

Ethnicity: Ethnic Somalis, 98.8 percent; Asian and Arab, 1.2 percent

Religion: 99 percent Muslim

Major languages: Somali, Arabic, English, Italian

SAMAALE CLAN DIVISION

Major clans

Darood	Isaaq	Hawiye	Dir	Rahanwin	Digil

Sub-clans

Ogaden	Habar Yoonis	Habar Gidir	Gadabursi
Majeerteen	Habar Awal	Abgaal	Iise
Mareenhaan	Habar Tol Jaalo	Biyamaal	
Dulbahante	Habar Jaalo	Hawaadle	
Warsangali	Iidagale	Murursade	
Yuusuf		Ujuuraan	
Kablalah			

GEOGRAPHY

Area: 246,201 square miles (686,803 sq km)

Highest point: Shimbir Berris, 7,897 feet (2,407 m)

Lowest point: Indian Ocean, sea level

Coastline: 1,880 miles (3,025 km.)

ECONOMY

(All monetary figures in U.S. dollars)

Currency: Somali shilling

Official exchange rate: 55 Somali shillings equal to $1

Per capita income: $300

Exports: livestock, animal products, gum, ghee, myrrh, frankincense, bananas

Imports: food products, grains, manufactured goods, machines

CHRONOLOGY

B.C.
ca. 100
Somalis leave their homeland in southern Ethiopia and gradually move southward to occupy modern Somalia.

A.D.
100
Somalis are established in southern Somalia and begin to move northward as their numbers increase.

600
Muslims from Saudi Arabia migrate to Somalia and the Horn of Africa to escape persecution at home.

900
Somalis, through contact with Saudi Muslims, convert en masse to the Islamic religion.

1854
British explorer Richard Burton leads an expedition into Somalia.

1884
Northern Somalia becomes a British protectorate.

1888
Southern Somalia becomes an Italian territory.

1897
Britain signs an agreement that gives the Ogaden region to Ethiopia.

1935
Italy invades and assumes control of Ethiopia.

1940
Italy moves into British Somaliland.

1941
Italy is defeated by British forces and is forced out of Somalia and Ethiopia; Britain administers both British and Italian Somaliland as well as the Ogaden region.

1947
Ogaden region is returned to Ethiopia.

1950
United Nations establishes a Trust territory in southern Somaliland and appoints Italy to oversee the territory with
the aim of granting the Somalis independence in ten years.

1955
Britain returns the Haud to Ethiopia.

1960
On June 26, Britain grants independence to its northern
Somali protectorate; on June 30, Italy grants southern So-
malia its independence; on July 1, northern and southern
Somaliland merge to form one nation—the Democratic
Republic of Somalia.

1961
First failed coup d'etat; the constitution is ratified.

1963
Britain cedes the Northern Frontier District to Kenya; first
unsuccessful rebellion in the Ogaden region.

1969
President Abdirashiid Ali Shemaarke is assassinated by one
of his guards; a successful military coup d'etat led by Major
General Siad Barre overthrows the democratically elected
government.

1970
French Somaliland is granted independence and votes to
become a separate nation, the Republic of Djibouti.

1972
A commission appointed by President Siad Barre establishes a standard script for the Somali language.

1974
Somalia becomes a member of the Arab League; literacy
campaign and International Women's Day launched.

1974–1975
Drought and the refugee problem intensify public dissatis-
faction with Siad Barre's regime.

1977
Somalia invades Ethiopia with the aim of regaining the Ogaden region.

1978
Somalia loses Ogaden War with Ethiopia.

1979
Somali Salvation Democratic Front formed with the purpose of overthrowing the government.

1981
Somali National Movement (SNM) formed with the purpose of overthrowing the government.

1988
SNM launches a major attack to take control of the northern region and is defeated through air bombardments by mercenaries and government supporters.

1989
United Somali Congress (USC) formed in the south to take over Mogadishu and force Siad Barre out.

1991
Siad Barre flees the capital after a bloody confrontation between government troops and armed members of the USC. Ali Madhi establishes an interim government for Somalia. The government is unrecognized by other political groups in Somalia. In May, SNM declares northern Somalia independent under the name of the Republic of Somaliland. Fighting in Mogadishu continues between different factions of the USC and other groups.

1992
Siad Barre is exiled to Nigeria; United Nations organizes a cease-fire in Mogadishu. Troops arrive in Somalia to keep the peace.

1993
United Nations troops pull out of Somalia. Fighting continues in Mogadishu.

1995
In January, Siad Barre dies in exile.

NOTES

INTRODUCTION: A LAND OF MANY CONTRADICTIONS

1. Quoted in Richard Burton, *First Footsteps in East Africa.* New York: Frederick A. Praegar, 1966, p. 25.

2. Burton, *First Footsteps in East Africa,* p. 93.

3. Quoted in Ruth Finnegan, ed., *A World Treasury of Oral Poetry.* Bloomington: Indiana University Press, 1978, pp. 107–108.

4. Ali Abdi, interview by author, Richmond, KY, April 24, 1999.

5. Said S. Samatar, *Oral Poetry and Somali Nationalism.* Cambridge: Cambridge University Press, 1982, p. 24.

CHAPTER 1: GEOGRAPHY

6. Quoted in John Middleton, ed., *Peoples of Africa: The Tribes and Cultures of an Intriguing Continent from Afrikaner to Zulu.* New York: Arco Publishing, 1978, p. 162.

CHAPTER 2: COLONIZATION

7. Quoted in Finnegan, ed., *A Treasury of Oral Poetry,* p. 119.

CHAPTER 3: THE PEOPLE AND THEIR SOCIETY

8. Abdi, interview.

9. David D. Laitin and Said S. Samatar, *Somalia: Nation in Search of a State.* Boulder, CO: Westview Press, 1987, p. 42.

10. Abdi, interview.

CHAPTER 4: SOMALI GOVERNMENT AND POLITICS: A QUEST FOR ORDER

11. Nuruddin Farah, "Savaging the Soul of a Nation," *The Writer in Politics,* 1996, p. 113.

12. Quoted in I. M. Lewis, *Blood and Bone: The Call of Kinship in Somali Society.* Lawrenceville, NJ: Red Sea Press, 1994, p. 169.

13. Lewis, *Blood and Bone,* p. 169.

CHAPTER 5: JUST GETTING BY: LIVING AND WORKING IN SOMALIA

14. B. W. Andrzejewski and I. M. Lewis, *Somali Poetry: An Introduction.* Oxford: Clarendon Press, 1964, p. 18.

15. Carol Beckwith and Angela Fisher, *African Ark: Peoples and Ancient Cultures of Ethiopia and the Horn of Africa.* New York: Harry N. Abrams, 1990, p. 146.

16. Ibrahim Ismaa'll, "An Early Somali Autobiography," *Africa,* 1997, vol. 2, p. 166.

CHAPTER 6: A RICH ARTISTIC HERITAGE

17. Quoted in B. W. Andrzejewski, "Reflections on the Nature and Social Function of Somali Proverbs," *African Language Review,* 1968, vol. 7, p. 74.

18. Andrzejewski, "Reflections on the Nature and Social Function of Somali Proverbs," p. 79.

19. Andrzejewski and Lewis, *Somali Poetry,* p. 45.

20. Abdi, interview.

21. Quoted in Samatar, *Oral Poetry,* p. 55.

22. Quoted in Andrzejewski and Lewis, *Somali Poetry,* p. 135.

23. Quoted in Beckwith and Fisher, *African Ark,* p. 149.

24. Quoted in Finnegan, *A Treasury of Oral Poetry,* p. 103.

25. Quoted in Finnegan, *A Treasury of Oral Poetry,* p. 107.

26. Quoted in Andrzejewski and Lewis, *Somali Poetry,* p. 140.

27. Quoted in Katheryne S. Loughran, et al., eds., *Somalia in Word and Image;* Washington, DC: Foundation for Cross Cultural Understanding, 1986, p. 31.

28. In Loughran, *Somalia in Word and Image,* p. 31.

SUGGESTIONS FOR FURTHER READING

Korwa G. Adar, *Kenyan Foreign Policy Behavior Towards Somalia, 1963–1983.* Lanham, MD: University Press of America, 1994. Gives a detailed account of the conflict between Kenya and Somalia over the Northern Frontier Province.

Africa Watch, *Somalia: A Government at War with Its Own People.* New York: Africa Watch, 1989. A powerful account of what happened in northern Somalia during the wars of the 1980s, the human rights abuses by the government, and the role the international community played in the final demise of the Somali state.

Harold Courlander, *The Fire on the Mountain.* New York: Holt, Rinehart and Winston, 1950. Contains many folktales from Ethiopia and Somalia.

Jama Mohamed Ghalib, *The Cost of Dictatorship: The Somali Experience.* New York: Lilian Barber Press, 1995. An account of the personal experiences of a Somali policeman during the repressive rule of Siad Barre and the collapse of the Somali state.

Patrick Gilkes, *Conflict in Somalia and Ethiopia.* New York: New Discovery Books, 1994. A highly readable book on the relationship between Ethiopia and Somalia. Discusses the historical sources of the conflict between Somalia and Ethiopia and the consequences of the conflict for both countries.

The Diagram Group, *Peoples of East of Africa.* New York: Facts On File, 1997. This book gives an enlightening description of the culture of various ethnic groups living in East Africa and their relationship to one another. The groups covered include the Somalis, Oromos, and Afars.

I. M. Lewis, *Saints and Somalis: Popular Islam in a Clan-Based Society.* Lawrence, NJ: Red Sea Press, 1998. This book gives an in-depth view of the history of Islam in Somalia and how Islamic values affect the lives of Somalis.

Terrece Lyons and Ahmed I. Samatar, *Somalia: State Collapse, Multilateral Intervention, and Strategies for Political Reconstruction.* Washington, DC: The Brookings Institution, 1995. A valuable book on the events that led to the collapse of the Somali state, and why the United Nations intervention failed.

J. Mattews, *I Remember Somalia.* Austin, TX: Raintree Steck-Vaughn Publishers, 1995. This books explains in simple terms the lives of Somali refugees and why they left Somalia. It also gives a nostalgic look at Somalia before the civil war.

WORKS CONSULTED

BOOKS

Hussein Adam and Richard Ford, *Removing Barricades in Somalia.* Washington, DC: United States Institute of Peace, 1998.

B. W. Andrzejewski and I. M. Lewis, *Somali Poetry: An Introduction.* Oxford: Clarendon Press, 1964. Valuable as one of the first books to present translations of Somali oral poems to the English-speaking world.

Carol Beckwith and Angela Fisher, *African Ark.* New York: Harry N. Abrams, 1990. A valuable book filled with photographs of the people living in the Horn of Africa.

Ralph E. Drake-Brockman, *British Somaliland.* London: Hurst & Blackett, 1912. Still considered a classic for its detailed description of northern Somalia during the British rule from the 1880s through 1960.

Richard Burton, *First Footsteps in East Africa.* New York: Frederick A. Praeger, 1966. Account of Somali people and culture by the first European to travel through the region.

Countries of the World and Their Leaders Yearbook 1999. Detroit: Gale Research. A compilation of the United States Reports. Offers valuable statistics on Somalia and other nations of the world.

Harold Courlander, *The King's Drum and Other African Stories.* New York: Harcourt, Brace & World, 1962. A collection of interesting African folktales.

———, *A Treasury of African Folklore.* New York: Crown Publishers, 1975. Presents African folk stories, epics, and wise sayings.

103

Ruth Finnegan, *A World Treasury of Oral Poetry.* Bloomington: Indiana University Press, 1978. Contains translations
of original poems from many countries of the world, including Somalia.

Robert L. Hess, *Italian Colonialism in Somalia.* Chicago:
University of Chicago Press, 1966. Gives a detailed description of the activities of the Italians in southern Somalia during the colonial rule.

Douglas Jardine, *The Mad Mullah of Somaliland.* New York:
Negro Universities Press, 1923. Offers the British account
of the character and activities of Mahammed Abdille Has-
san, the Dervish leader that led a twenty-one-year guerilla
attack on the colonizing forces in Somalia.

David D. Laitin, *Politics, Language, and Thought: The Somali
Experience.* Chicago: University of Chicago Press, 1977. A
valuable book on the political, social, and linguistic aspects of Somali society.

David D. Laitin and Said S. Samatar, *Somalia: Nation in
Search of a State.* Boulder, CO: Westview Press, 1987. Discusses the political culture of Somali society.

I. M. Lewis, *A Pastoral Democracy.* New York: African Publishing Company, 1982. A valuable book on the social and
political aspects of life in northern Somalia.

———, *Blood and Bone: The Call of Kinship in Somali Society.* Lawrenceville, NJ: Red Sea Press, 1994. A valuable
book on kinship relationships in Somalia. It details how
clan association controls all aspect of Somali life, including the present collapse of the Somali state.

Katheryne S. Loughran, et al., eds., *Somalia in Word and Image.* Washington, DC: Foundation for Cross Cultural Understanding, 1986. A scholarly book on the literature and
art of Somalia. Contains useful pictures.

John Markakis, *National and Class Conflict in the Horn of
Africa.* Cambridge: Cambridge University Press, 1987. Details the sources of the conflict between Somalia and
other nations of the Horn of Africa.

John Middleton, ed., *Peoples of Africa: The Tribes and Cultures of an Intriguing Continent from Afrikaner to Zulu.*

New York: Arco Publishing, 1978. Gives brief overviews of most ethnic groups in Africa. Color pictures.

Helen Chapin Metz, ed., *Somalia: A Country Study.* Washington, DC: Federal Research Division, Library of Congress, 1993. Offers a full-length study of all aspects of Somali culture until 1991.

Sean Moroney, ed., *Handbooks to the Modern Word: Africa.* Vol. 1. New York: Facts On File, 1989. Offers valuable statistics.

Christian P. Potholm, *Four African Political Systems.* Englewood Cliffs, New Jersey: Prentice-Hall, 1970. Describes the political structure of Somali society until 1969.

Saadia Touval. *Somali Nationalism.* Cambridge, MA: Harvard University Press, 1963. A valuable book on the Somali political culture during and after colonial rule.

Marlita A. Reddy, ed., *Statistical Abstract of the World.* New York: Gale Research, 1994. Gives valuable statistics.

Mohammed Sahnoun, *Somalia: The Missed Opportunities.* Washington, DC: United States Institute of Peace Press, 1994. Recounts the experiences of a United Nations envoy to Somalia in 1992 and details the lessons Somalia teaches the world about the most effective way to handle international crises.

Said S. Samatar, *Oral Poetry and Somali Nationalism.* Cambridge: Cambridge University Press, 1982. Explicates the poetry of Sayyid Muhammad ibn AbdAllah Hasan and discusses how Somali poetry is used to discuss and record every aspect of the Somali experience.

Articles

M. H. Abdulaziz, "Language in Education: A Comparative Study of the Situation in Tanzania, Ethiopia and Somalia," *Bilingual Education.* Vol. 1 Ed. by Ofelia Garcia. Philadelphia: John Benjamins Publishing Company, 1991. The essay discusses educational issues in Somalia.

Ali Jimale Ahmed, "Of Poets and Sheikhs: Somali Literature," *Faces of Islam in African Literature,* ed. by Kenneth W.

Harrow. Portsmouth, NH: Heinemann, 1991. Discusses how poets and sheihs (Muslim leaders) are important to Somali literature and society.

B. W. Andrzejewski and Musa H. I. Galaal, "A Somali Poetic Combat," *Journal of African Languages,* vol. 2, 1963. Contains a series of three long poems, recited by three great Somali poets, Ali Duuh, Qamaan Bulhan, and Salaan Arrabey, in a polemical exchange.

B. W. Andrzejewski, "Reflections on the Nature and Social Function of Somali Proverbs," *African Language Review,* vol. 7, 1968. Gives a good discussion on the functions of proverbs in Somali society.

Nuruddin Farah, "Savaging the Soul of a Nation," *The Writer in Politics,* 1996. Recounts the personal experiences of this internationally known Somali writer in response to the events leading to the total collapse of the Somali state in 1991.

Zainab Mohamed Jama, "Fighting to be Heard: Somali Women's Poetry," *African Language and Cultures,* vol. 4, no. 1, 1991. Discusses the place of women's literature within Somali culture.

Ibrahim Ismaa'il, "An Early Somali Autobiography," annotated by Richard Pankhurst, *Africa,* vol. 2, 1977. Gives an interesting account of the life of the author as he struggles to grow up as a nomad in Somalia.

INTERVIEWS

Ali Abdi. Interview by author. Richmond, KY, April 24, 1999.

Timothy Kiogora. Interview by author. Richmond, KY, April 10, 1999.

INDEX

107

PICTURE CREDITS

ABOUT THE AUTHOR

Salome C. Nnoromele is a native of Nigeria. She received her undergraduate degree from the University of Utah in Salt Late City. Her master's and doctorate degrees are from the University of Kentucky. She is currently associate professor of English at Eastern Kentucky University. She is the author of *Life Among the Ibo Women of Nigeria* and several essays on African culture and literature.